Roy Stone

New Roads and Road Laws in the United States

Roy Stone

New Roads and Road Laws in the United States

ISBN/EAN: 9783744678667

Printed in Europe, USA, Canada, Australia, Japan

Cover: Foto ©ninafisch / pixelio.de

More available books at **www.hansebooks.com**

NEW ROADS AND ROAD LAWS

IN THE

UNITED STATES

BY

ROY STONE

VICE-PRESIDENT NATIONAL LEAGUE FOR GOOD ROADS, AND U. S. SPECIAL AGENT
AND ENGINEER FOR ROAD INQUIRY, DEPARTMENT OF AGRICULTURE

NEW YORK
D. VAN NOSTRAND COMPANY
23 MURRAY AND 27 WARREN STREETS
1894

PREFACE.

The greater portion of the material for this work was gathered before the establishment of the Government Inquiry into "Systems of Road Management in the United States," and when the writer took charge of that inquiry, it was thought best, in view of the urgent demand for a publication of this character and the delay involved in organizing the inquiry and making a proper digest of its results for publication, to carry out the original intention, and publish, in a private form, the information already at hand, and such additional matter as might come in through the inquiry or otherwise during the preparation of the volume for the press. In addition to supplying a present need, it is hoped that this book may still further stimulate public interest in the subject, and thus promote the success of the official inquiry.

The demand for information on this subject generally relates —

First, To the new legislation for road improvement and the working of that legislation;

Second, To the cost and methods of road construction;

Third, To the effects of road improvement where it has been accomplished.

PREFACE.

Until the organization of the National League for Good Roads, no serious attempt appears to have been made to gather this information in the United States.

By means of the Consular Reports a knowledge of foreign road-making has been widely spread, but the densest ignorance still prevails in respect to our home efforts and their results.

This work attempts only to give a condensed account of recent progress in American road-making, with details of the examples which have been most conspicuously successful, together with some suggestions for legislation and for road construction.

New developments succeed each other rapidly in this field; since the body of this book was in type, committees of the New York State Legislature and Boards of Supervisors have visited the State Aid Road Districts of New Jersey, and on their return have passed a State Aid law through the lower house by a vote of four to one.

This visit and its result have been widely discussed, and another winter will see a movement for State Aid in many States; for the visitors have spread far and wide the news of farming communities actually getting rich in these hard times, and attributing their prosperity entirely to their good roads.

ROY STONE.

WASHINGTON, D.C., May 4, 1894.

CONTENTS.

CHAPTER		PAGE
I.	Recent Progress in Road Improvement	1
II.	The Government Road Inquiry	19
III.	The New Roads of Canandaigua, N.Y.	35
IV.	Modern Kentucky Road-Building	43
V.	Connecticut Roads	46
VI.	Cheap Stone Roads in Virginia, Michigan, New Jersey, and Maryland	50
VII.	Ineffective County Road Laws. — Local Option Law of New Jersey	55
VIII.	Proposed Amendments to the New Jersey Road Law	59
IX.	Further Modification of the Same Law suggested	62
X.	State Aid, and the Method of giving it	69
XI.	Another Form of State Aid. — Convict Labor	74
XII.	What the Railroads will do for the Highways	81
XIII.	Road Materials in the United States	87
XIV.	The Best Road for a Farming District	91
XV.	The Best Construction for a Narrow Hard Road. — Some Farm Roads in Illinois	94
XVI.	Treatment of Sandy Roads	97
XVII.	Treatment of Dirt Roads	101
XVIII.	Wide Tires	103
XIX.	The Report of the Ohio Road Commission	109
XX.	Farmers and the Roads	114
XXI.	The Wheelmen's Campaign for Roads	118
XXII.	The Attitude of Commercial Organizations	120
XXIII.	Road-Building and the Revival of Business	123

APPENDIX.

	PAGE
Abstracts of New Road Laws in Sixteen States	139
Proposed Law for State Aid in New York	147
Proposed State Aid in Pennsylvania . . .	151
State Highway Commission. Law of Massachusetts, 1893 . .	154
State Engineer Department. Law proposed by the Maryland Road League	161
Free Road Materials by Convict Labor.	
1. Laws of Delaware, Chap. 670, 1893 .	163
2. Proposed Law in Iowa	166

LIST OF ILLUSTRATIONS.

	FACING PAGE
Stone Road, Canandaigua, N.Y.	35
Canandaigua Roads	40
Mud Road at End of Stone Road, Canandaigua, N.Y.	43
Country Road, Alexandria County, Va.	50
Washington and Alexandria Turnpike, March, 1894	54
Church Road, Camden County, N.J.	62
Transverse Sections of New Jersey Telford Roads	66
Church Road, Camden County, N.J., before Macadamizing	68
Road-Building in North Carolina, Blowing up Stumps	80
Cross-Sections of Narrow Stone Roads	96
Judge Caton's Farm Roads in Illinois	97
Church Road, One Mile East of Merchantville	114
Farm Teams on their Way to Market	117
Road-Building in North Carolina	123

CHAPTER I.

RECENT PROGRESS IN ROAD IMPROVEMENT.

The task of transforming a million miles, or more, of bad roads into good ones, a task which involved the disruption of century old systems, the development of new lines of legislation in all the States of our Union, and, in many, even the changing of their constitutions, and which has threatened to require an expenditure running into billions, has commonly been deemed so vast and difficult as to be utterly hopeless; but it suddenly appears that the few good citizens who have had the courage to attempt it, here and there, have reason to be astonished at their own success. Not only have the ways and means been found without oppression to the taxpayer, but the actual cost of good road-making has been brought far below the early estimates. Sixteen States have passed new road laws, more or less radical in their nature, and one has amended its constitution to permit the adoption of such laws. Many hundreds of miles of good roads have already been built, in localities widely separated, under varying conditions and through various methods of administration, finance, and construction.

It is therefore no longer necessary to go abroad for instruction in this reform, but, on the other hand, highly necessary to learn what is being done at home; the country is so vast, that what is done and well done in one section is often unknown or misunderstood in another, and each community has, so far as regards the experience of others, wrought mostly in the dark. Some recent developments of the road movement tend, however, toward a thorough investigation of the subject, and a wide diffusion of the knowledge so gained.

In Chicago a year ago last October, in the midst of the universal excitement and enthusiasm which attended the opening ceremonies of the Great Fair, and the dedication of the White City, a representative body of men coming from all parts of the land, and from every walk in life, drew aside from the contemplation of the triumphs of American civilization to counsel together on one great reproach to that civilization, — the condition of the common roads of the country. In this gathering there were delegates from all the existing State organizations for road improvement, from many Boards of Trade and Agriculture, from Agricultural Colleges and Universities, and from Farmers' Clubs and Wheelmen's Leagues, besides many individual leaders in the general movement. No more harmonious assemblage ever discussed a public question. Each speaker presented only a varied phase of the same picture of the country's need and its opportunity.

One said: "*Columbus discovered America in vain if, after four hundred years, we are still behind the ancient*

Peruvians in one of the elements of civilization, and are not ashamed of it; a people not yet emerged from barbarism, with no written language, and no means of record or communication better than a knotted string, yet possessing a system of roads which astonished their Spanish conquerors more than all the other marvels of that marvellous land."

"A Spanish writer of the day pictured the Great Road from Quito to Cuzco in this lofty language: 'I believe that in all the history of man there has been no account of such grandeur as is to be seen in this road, which passes over deep valleys and lofty mountains, by snowy heights, over falls of water, through live rocks, and along the edges of furious torrents; in all places level and paved; along mountain slopes terraced; through the living rock cut; along the river banks supported by walls; in the snowy heights with steps and resting-places; in all parts ten paces wide, clean swept, clear of stones, and, at intervals, post-houses and storehouses and temples of the Sun.'"

Another speaker said: "*A strange apathy has fallen upon the country, and a strange paralysis upon the government, since the time when the Fathers of the Republic declared it the duty of Congress to bind the Republic together with roads and canals.*"

A well-known Western editor said: "The building of the needed highways of the land is of no less consequence to America in the development of its resources than the building of its 200,000 miles of railroad. Fortunately for all interests involved the magnitude of the undertaking does not appall any one, but the whole country, without excepting the smallest fragment, favors the good work. There is not an institution of learning, from the highest university to the primary school, but teachers and pupils favor good roads. If money talks, every dollar in the land is speaking a good word for better roads. It is an object which permeates all society, without room for an unfriendly thought. It concerns every phase of religious belief, but steers clear of sectarianism. It takes complete possession of all politics, but avoids all parties. In a word, the continent is solid for good roads."

"How shall they be built? To answer this, the most important question which can come before the American people in the next century is the scope, object, and purpose of the National Road League which this National Convention is assembled to organize."

The Secretary of the Iowa Road Improvement Association, after describing the waste and losses due to bad roads, said: "Build permanent country roads, passable during twelve months in the year, and these adverse conditions disappear. The farmer sells his grain or stock when prices tempt him; he delivers when his other duties permit without sacrifice of time; he buys his supplies on rainy days, emancipated from the spasmodic and uncertain market; he reforms his methods and the character of his farming, raising a greater variety of crops, fruits, vegetables, and dairy products, many of them perishable with uncertain and bad roads, but profitable with good roads open every day in the year.

His lands, as a result of this diversity in farming, increase in fertility and in value, and he becomes a prosperous social being.

"The merchant can then engage in business with less capital and can carry smaller stocks of goods. He ceases to become an enforced money-lender to the farmer, as he is when he sells on credit, and in turn he meets his own obligations promptly and in cash. The manufacturer and jobber distribute throughout the year instead of in seasons, thereby releasing much of their capital for other enterprises. The railroad company cuts down its investment in useless rolling-stock, if freed from the congestion of spasmodic transportation, and performs its duties toward its patrons without friction, promptly and efficiently, and with the resultant good-will of the entire public."

The President of the American Bankers' Association said: "The distressingly improvident and wasteful condition of the common roads of the United States, that are quagmires half of the year and beds of dust the other half, and the great necessity for their improvement, are becoming universally recognized. The people are at last beginning to realize that bad roads annually entail losses that in magnitude are beyond computation, and that their permanent improvement would yearly affect the saving of untold millions to the nation.

"There is no man, woman, or child in the land that has not a personal interest in the question of better roads. There is no article produced, imported, or exported, the cost of which is not in some degree affected by the character of the common roads over which it is transported from the field, the mine, the mill, or the ship, to the user or consumer; and the worse the roads over which it is transported, the less it yields the producer, and the more it costs the user or consumer; and the loss thus borne year after year by the entire people of the nation is so enormous that it cannot even be reasonably approximated.

"While the vast improvement and extensions of railways, and the increase in number, size, and means of propulsion of vessels have reduced the cost of transportation by rail and water to a minimum, the cost of transportation over our common roads means practically the same at near the close of the world's greatest century of progress in other means of transportation as it was at its beginning. It costs less to transport commodities across the continent by rail, or from continent to continent by water, than it does over a single mile of some of our common roads during nearly half the year."

The outcome of this notable gathering was the inception of the NATIONAL LEAGUE FOR GOOD ROADS, and that organization was so well established by the following winter that it was able to hold a convention in Washington, with more than half the States of the Union represented.

The Press of the country was constant and earnest in its aid of the movement, its columns containing many such articles as the following:—

"The National League for Good Roads is wasting no

time nor letting any circumstance delay its work. Amid the tumult of the Columbian celebration at Chicago it brought together a large and interested body of practical men for formal organization; and to-day, amid the culminating excitement of the presidential campaign, its executive committee meets in this capital to perfect plans for extending its work immediately into every school district of the United States. The object of the League should enlist the sympathy and co-operation, as its personal composition commands the confidence, of all public-spirited citizens; without which, indeed, its success will not be easily attained. To provide the nation with good roads is a stupendous undertaking; but, in the way the League indicates, it can be accomplished, and it should be and must be accomplished." — *N. Y. Tribune.*

"It is a remarkable evidence of the hold which the good roads reform has upon the American people, that in the midst of the absorbing festivities of Columbus week it was possible to hold a large and enthusiastic meeting at Chicago in its interests. The gathering at Central Music Hall contained prominent representatives of many States and many industries from East and West, North and South. To the promoters of the good roads movement is due the honor of inaugurating a reform which is bound before long to enlist the best and most powerful elements of our population." — *Chicago Post.*

"Good roads mean blessings of untold value to all sections where bad roads are at present the rule. The improvement of the public highways will tend to largely augment the benefit of railway communication, will bring the farmers and merchants into closer relations, will shorten the distance to markets, will save an immense amount of wear and tear to vehicles and stock, will help trade, help commerce, help education, help investments, help everything that conduces to the material welfare of the people. All honor and success, therefore, to the proposed national organization."—*Washington Post.*

The Washington Convention aroused the strongest interest and sympathy in all departments of the government; and many senators, members of Congress, and executive officials attended and took part in the deliberations.

Senator Manderson, President of the National League, said: "It would be waste of time for any one in this presence to speak of the necessity for the work that we are engaged in. I know of no subject more important than the bettering of the roads of the United States. No detailed statement of the deplorable existing condition is necessary. We know the fact that we must get out of the present methods and mend our ways the country over. We can congratulate ourselves that there is such widespread interest on the subject of educating the people for their own good. The newspapers all over have taken up the matter and have created such interest that in some localities better roads have already resulted. It was a source of very great pleasure to me that in the county of Douglas, in which

I live, in the State of Nebraska, largely as the result of the agitation of this question by the newspapers, the people have already started to build better roads, and have in that county voted $150,000, to be issued in bonds, the proceeds to be expended for that purpose. This experience has been repeated all over the land."

Among the remarks made by other speakers were the following: —

By Senator Chandler: "Mr. Chairman and gentlemen of the National League for Good Roads: I am glad to say a few words on this important subject. It is one that deeply interests my own State. I am here at the request of Governor John B. Smith, who has just been inaugurated, and of Ex-Governors David H. Goodell (vice-president of your League for the State of New Hampshire) and Hiram A. Tuttle, all of whom take a warm interest in this subject.

"The question of good roads in New Hampshire has connected itself with that of forestry, because, in order to keep New Hampshire prominent, as we know it now is, among the summer resorts of the United States, it is necessary for us not only to have good highways and good roads, giving easy access to our natural scenery, but we must preserve our forests and our watercourses.

"Now, the first thing that we have thought of has been to abolish working out the taxes, because the towns do not get full advantage of the money that is voted under the existing system. We expect to be instructed by the National League for Good Roads as to other measures for improving the roads of our State."

Regarding action by Congress, the Senator said: "Therefore, gentlemen, state what you want Congress to do. Either a national commission should be appointed, or the Secretary of Agriculture should be authorized to make investigation and ascertain the needs of the country and the best methods of improving our roads, and the aid of the National Government should be in other ways invoked to arouse our people to the necessities which are upon the country in connection with improving roads. Beyond that, as to what should be asked of Congress, I desire to be instructed. I know I express the sentiment, not only of myself, but of the chairman, Senator Manderson, and of General P. S. Post, whom I see here, and of many other senators and representatives, when I say that if you will state in what way you think the aid of Congress ought to be invoked in this work, assuming the request to be reasonable, we will do all we can to assist in accomplishing your wishes."

By the Secretary of Agriculture, Hon. J. M. Rusk: "The U. S. Department of Agriculture is in full sympathy with this movement. It ought to be, as the national representative of the agricultural interest. A dollar saved in transportation is a dollar added to net production. What shall the farmer do with his surplus product, and why raise this surplus, if his way to the outside world is barred by impassable highways, or obstructed by obstacles which increase threefold the expense of realizing the fruits of his industry? Can we enlighten him by showing him a better way of expending the taxes levied upon him for the improvement of his roads? Can we show him such a system, well driven home with clear persuasion and positive assurances, as will induce him to take hold of the subject with energy? I believe that the time is ripe to submit this matter to the intelligence of the American public. There should be a unity of interest between the city and the country. The city is almost as much interested in getting good roads as the country itself. To the country it means enhanced net value to country products; to the city it means a greater variety and no essential increase in cost to the consumer.

"No one man can improve the highways of a neighborhood. All must act together in behalf of their common interest, and people in yielding something to the common interest will in the end, by intelligent co-operation and systematic methods, be the recipients of benefits far beyond any possible results arising from discordant and uncompromising individual demands. Every person must be brought to see this and be induced to yield his individual interest to a wider range of road improvement, and to a single system wider than the horizon as seen from his own doorstep."

By Major Sanger, U.S.A.: "I am not a delegate to this convention, but the representative, by proxy, of a relative, who is a delegate from the State of New York. I have taken advantage, however, of my temporary connection with the convention to bring the objects of the Road League to the notice of the military authorities in Washington, and it affords me much pleasure to say that both the Secretary of War and the Major-General Commanding the Army are in full sympathy with this movement in behalf of good country roads, not only because of their great value to military operations, should they ever be necessary, but because of their effect generally, in facilitating intercourse in those sections where railroads and telegraphs are not relied on, as yet, for communication. I have been requested by the Secretary and by General Schofield to assure the convention of their wish to co-operate with all the means at their disposal, and to request the convention to point out to them in what way this can be done so as to best promote the objects of the League. General Schofield has given the subject of roads much consideration, more especially those along our Canadian border, on both sides of the line, and fully appreciates their importance, no matter in what part of the country they may be situated. As you are doubtless aware, the army has been for years the pioneer of Western emigration in this country, and by its marches and the posts it has built has been largely instrumental in determining the sites of our Western cities and the main lines of communication between them. It is my belief that the intelligence and experience of the army can be made a valuable auxiliary in the establishment of good roads, and I am quite sure, from what the military authorities have said, that they would be glad to use them for that purpose."

By Judge Thayer, President of Iowa State Road Association: "This great uprising is not local. It is as broad as the continent and foreshadows the grandest moral and physical revolution that ever aroused a civilized people. It means a nation stirred up from centre to circumference.

"It may be that a higher education in road-making is essential to a proper comprehension of the movement which is covering the land. But I cannot believe that is the case. Never since the foundation stone of yonder Capitol was laid has there been any long-continued period but object lessons in bad road-making were as familiar to the person who walked or drove a team as is the plough to the husbandman. Those object lessons exist to-day all over this broad land, in front of every farmer's dooryard, and they keep him company on every journey he makes to the village or to the church; they stare at him with a ghostly glare when he takes his dead to the burying-ground, and his little children trudge homeward from the schoolhouse with those lessons the most impressive of all they learn.

"I believe the education is complete. Every man has his fill. He has drank deep at the fountain of that kind of knowledge. Now he is prepared for reform, and if he is ready to get out of the rut as well as the mud, this earthquake which is waking people up will keep them awake until the good roads become object lessons that put the finest paintings in the shade, and the bad roads become forever obsolete.

"The education complete, then comes practical road-making. What is it? How is it done? I am confident that to carry on road-making on an **extensive** scale as would be wise or prudent will not require an increase of taxation. The average taxpayer has a greater horror of adding more taxes to his burdens than he has of adding to his roads more mud. He will be an enthusiast in favor of better roads; he will take a front seat at road meetings and applaud every reference to road reform, but when it comes to suggesting more taxes he feels like rising up, taking his hat, and hunting a little fresh air. He is no longer in it. He wants to be counted out. Nor do I blame him. Not that taxes are unreasonably high, considering the blessings and advantages the people derive from the institutions of the land, which must flourish to a certain extent by means of taxation, but in this matter of good road taxes he has gotten into a rut, and nothing so nicely fits the wheel as the rut; and unless there is something just as good, without additional time, trouble, or expense to reach it, he prefers to jog along in the old groove to the end of the chapter or the road. But fortunately the taxpayer can throw up both hands for road improvements and enter the arena of road reform with his coat off and his heart and hands earnestly in the work, and be satisfied without a scruple of doubt that the better roads the whole country is advocating may come with taxation reduced rather than increased.

"Not only must there be a radical change in the manner of paying road taxes, but the money thus paid must be expended in a different way. The local method of building roads must in a great measure be abandoned. The next generation must be asked to help bear the expense of building the roads which the next generation will enjoy. To do this, the road taxes need not be increased, but use the taxes to pay the interest on loans for money advanced to build good roads economically and on an extensive scale.

"Construct roads on the same plan whereby the great enterprises of this land have been built up. If it is thought the best policy to limit road-building to a county, and not make the State the chief factor, provide that all the road taxes shall be paid into the treasury, and, instead of being used in the repairing of the roads already built, devote the larger portion to building permanent roads and the rest to repairs. If there should be a prejudice in any county against borrowing money on long-time bonds at a low rate of interest and spending the money as rapidly as it can be done to advantage, and using the taxes to pay the interest and creating a sinking fund to pay the principal when due, then adopt a plan for building, with the annual taxes, a certain number of miles of good road every year. Different communities will have different views as to which policy it is best to pursue. But it is well enough to bear in mind that the larger number of the great improvements in this country have been brought about on borrowed money. One man never undertakes to build a railroad. For one man, or even one community, to undertake to build so much of a railroad as runs through his or its school district would be a slow method of building trunk lines of railroads. It might be done that way in time, but railroads have not been constructed in that way. The vast railroad system of this country is the work of the ablest financial geniuses, the best skilled engineers, the most successful business men the century has produced, and I believe that to-day, without loans on bonds, there would be less than 20,000 miles of road where there are 200,000 miles. Other great industries conducted on a colossal scale, and which are the pride and boast of the nation, owe their success to a combination of purses advancing money to be repaid in the future.

"So it is no unexplored field I take the public into when I ask it to enter upon a system of road-making that shall equal any undertaking in which the country has ever engaged, not excepting the building of nearly 200,000 miles of railroad.

"With the work undertaken on a large scale, the railroads will become an important factor in road-making, as it would be to their interest to haul the material at the cost of the service. The prison labor could be utilized, because it would pay the State to put the prisoners at work at such places where stone quarries were extensive, or at points where stone in the rough could be delivered at nominal cost, and make them central points from which the railroads would distribute the broken stone into sections of the State where there are no such quarries.

"Western cities are engaged in a general system of paving streets. They would not do this in any other way than the issuing of improvement bonds to run several years. The burden falls lightly on the shoulders of each property-owner, and the cities have the use of the paved streets years in advance of the all-cash-down system.

"But the cities are as much interested as the country in good roads, and they are willing to bear a share of such improvements. In order that they should have an opportunity to help on the work, the State should all the more contribute a certain amount for each mile of standard road built to be paid out of the general fund."

The Committee on Agriculture of the House of Representatives, being invited to meet the convention, sent the following reply:—

"COMMITTEE ON AGRICULTURE,
"HOUSE OF REPRESENTATIVES, U.S.
"Washington, D.C., January 18, 1893.

"GEN. ROY STONE,
 "General Vice-President and Secretary:

"SIR: Replying to your kind invitation to attend your conference at 11 A.M. of this date, the Committee on Agriculture are compelled to decline on account of lack of time. At some future time we hope to be able to attend; and at to-morrow's session at 11 o'clock the committee by unanimous vote extend an invitation to representatives of the National League for Good Roads to be present, and present the matter in any way they may deem proper.

"Very respectfully,
"W. H. HATCH,
"Chairman Committee on Agriculture."

Agreeably to this invitation, a large delegation waited upon the Committee; the subject of national aid to the movement was fully discussed, and, as a result, the Committee inserted in their appropriation bill the following item: —

"To enable the Secretary of Agriculture to make inquiries in regard to the systems of road management throughout the United States, to make investigations in regard to the best method of road-making, to prepare publications on this subject suitable for distribution; and to enable him to assist the agricultural colleges and experiment stations in disseminating information on this subject, ten thousand dollars ($10,000)."

This appropriation becoming available at the beginning of the present fiscal year, the Secretary of Agriculture on the 3d of October, 1893, instituted the office of Road Inquiry, by the appointment of a special agent and engineer to carry out the wishes of Congress in the matter.

CHAPTER II.

THE GOVERNMENT ROAD INQUIRY.

Upon his appointment, the officer in charge of the Road Inquiry received the following instructions:—

"SIR: You have been this day appointed to supervise and carry out the investigation pursuant to the Statute approved March 3, 1893, which has four branches:—

"*First:* To make inquiries in regard to the systems of road management throughout the United States.

"*Second:* To make investigations in regard to the best method of road-making.

"*Third:* To prepare didactic publications on this subject, suitable for publication.

"*Fourth:* To assist the agricultural colleges and experiment stations in disseminating information on this subject.

"It will not be profitable to enter upon all of these points at first. The work under the appropriation will need to be of gradual growth, conducted at all times economically. Therefore it is not expected that there will be any considerable force of clerical help, and, aside from your salary, no considerable expenditure for the present. It is understood that you have at your command, the data for a compilation of the laws of several of the States, upon which their road systems are based. It should be your first duty, therefore, to make such collection complete, and prepare a bulletin on that subject.

"Incidentally, while preparing this bulletin, you should charge yourself with collecting data relating to different methods of road-making, which, in the first instance, should be generic in their character; including, —

"*First:* The best method of constructing a common highway, without gravel or stone.

"*Second:* Gravel highways.

"*Third:* Macadam, and other stone roads.

"*Fourth:* Data upon which to base suggestions for the transportation of material within reasonable access, for the proper surfacing of the road-bed. These data should form the foundation for the second bulletin, or second series of bulletins.

"There are certain restrictions I wish specifically to bring to your attention. It must be borne in mind that the actual expense in the construction of these highways is to be borne by the localities and States in which they lie. Moreover, it is not the province of this Department to seek to control or influence said action, except in so far as advice and wise suggestions shall contribute toward it. This Department is to form no part of any plan, scheme, or organization, or to be a party to it in any way, which has for its object the concerted effort to secure and furnish labor to unemployed persons, or to convicts. These are matters to be carried on by States, localities, or charities. The Department is to furnish information, not to direct and formulate any system of organization, however efficient or desirable it may be. Any such effort on its part would soon make it subject to hostile criticism. You will publish this letter in the preface to your first bulletin.

"Yours truly,
"J. STERLING MORTON,
"*Secretary.*"

Upon receipt of these instructions letters of inquiry were prepared and sent: —

1. To the Governors of all the States and Territories, as follows: —

"The Congress of the United States having made provision" (here follows the appropriation as above). "I have the honor to request your Excellency's aid and co-operation in inaugurating this important inquiry.

"The information regarding foreign roads and road-making gathered by the Department of State through its consular representatives has proved to be of great value, and a corresponding home inquiry should be even more profitable. So many States and communities are attempting road improvement, and so many others are considering it, that a definite knowledge of what each has proposed or accomplished might be invaluable to many of the others. Such knowledge can be practically reached and disseminated only through a central agency, but that agency will need the assistance of all the State and local officials concerned, in order to bring its work within the means allotted by Congress and within a proper limit of time.

"The officer in charge of the inquiry has therefore been instructed to communicate with the Secretaries of State of the several States on the subject, and the Department would respectfully ask your Excellency, if it meets with your approval, to give your sanction to his requests, together with such voluntary aid as it may be in your power to give or procure, and will be further indebted to you for any recommendations or suggestions regarding sources of information or the scope of the inquiry itself, which is yet somewhat undefined.

"I have the honor to remain, Sir,
"Yours very respectfully,
"(*Signed*) EDWIN WILLITS,
"*Acting Secretary.*"

2. To the Secretaries of State: —

"SIR: The act of Congress making appropriations for this Department for the current fiscal year contains the following provision: —

"To enable" (etc., as before).

"The scope of this inquiry corresponds closely with that of the one successfully made by the State Department, through its consular representatives, into the road laws and methods of road construction in foreign countries.

"The success and value of a home inquiry will

depend much upon the aid given it by the various State and local officials who have been concerned in road improvement. I have the honor, therefore, to request your co-operation in this important work, to the extent at least of furnishing the names of all such officials, and of any individuals who may in your judgment be able to give valuable information or suggestions pertaining to the subject.

"I take leave also to ask for copies of all recent laws or compilations of laws bearing upon roads and highways.

"As the inquiry progresses, the Department will furnish you with copies of all published results."

3. To Members of Congress: —

"DEAR SIR: In pursuing the inquiry into 'systems of road management' and 'methods of road-making,' authorized by the Fifty-second Congress, the Department of Agriculture desires to communicate on the subject with the best-informed authorities and private individuals throughout the United States, and, to expedite the matter, I have the honor to request your aid in procuring the names of all counties or townships in your district which have made a systematic attempt at modern road improvement, and also the names and addresses of the officials and of some of the individuals most actively concerned in such improvement, whether in respect to legislation or road construction.

"If you are personally interested in the subject, I

shall be glad to receive any further information or suggestions from you pertaining to the inquiry."

4. To the State Geologists:—

"Dear Sir: The U. S. Department of Agriculture has been assured of the general and hearty co-operation of the State Governments in the inquiry authorized by Congress 'into the systems of road management and the best methods of road construction throughout the United States'; and as one of the most important branches of the inquiry relates to *road materials*, and thereby comes within your province, I take leave to ask for such information on that head as you may be able to give — having in view the supply not only of your own, but of adjacent States — if you have material of superior quality. The general use of the highest class of materials involves the cost of railway transportation for most of them, but the Department is already assured by many of the railway companies of their disposition to accord extremely low rates on such traffic, for the encouragement of road-building; and if this action becomes general, a haul of one hundred, or even two hundred miles, may not be prohibitory, so that the very best roads may be built in regions which have no local supply of material.

"I send, herewith, the general circular of inquiry, and shall be glad to receive any information you may be able to give or obtain on other branches of the subject."

5. To Railroad Presidents: —

"SIR: The Department of Agriculture has been authorized by Congress to make inquiry into the systems of road management throughout the United States, and the best methods of road-making, and to collect and distribute information regarding the same.

"The interest uniformly shown by railway managers in the improvement of highways warrants the Department, which has been charged with this inquiry, in asking their assistance. The undersigned, therefore, respectfully requests: (1) Such information as can be gained through your engineering department regarding the supply of good road materials along or near your lines — their location, character, accessibility, and the cost of preparation and loading on cars; (2) Your schedule rates for transportation of the same; (3) A statement of any reduced rates or free transportation that may have been granted or offered in special cases to encourage road-building; (4) Any information, recommendations, or suggestions from yourself, or any of your staff, that may promote the success of this inquiry or the general interest of road improvement."

6. General circular of inquiry: —

"The Department of Agriculture, being charged by Congress with an inquiry into the systems of road management and the best methods of road construction throughout the United States, desires information upon the following points: —

"1. The practical working of the recent road laws of the various States, wherever the same have been tested; the difficulties found in their application, and suggestions for their amendment.

"2. The character and cost of the roads built under these laws, the materials used, and the present condition and prospective durability of such roads.

"3. The location and character of any superior stone for roads which is accessible by railway or water, the cost of quarrying, preparing, and loading the same, the mileage rates of transportation, and any instances of reduced or free transportation given by railways for the encouragement of road-building.

"4. The same information, so far as applicable, regarding materials naturally prepared, such as the Paducah and Tishomingo gravels, the Hamilton sandstones, and the Chickamauga flints.

"5. The results of any experiments in the construction of narrow and cheap hard roads, or of roads having one track of earth and one of stone or gravel, with full particulars as to cost and method of construction.

"6. The result of any practical experience in the use of burnt clay for roads.

"7. The cost and benefits of tile drainage of roads, as shown by practice.

"8. The best method of constructing a common highway without gravel or stone, and with or without under-drainage.

"9. Definite facts as to the enhancement of property values through road improvement.

"10. The results of any experiments in the employment of convict labor on roads or the preparation of road materials.

"11. The details of all bond issues for road improvement, and how, where, and at what cost the bonds were marketed.

"12. The rates allowed in each State for men and teams in working out road taxes, and the actual value of such work as compared with labor paid for in cash.

"All communications should be addressed to 'Office of Road Inquiry, U. S. Department of Agriculture, Washington, D.C.'"

A brief summary of the operations of the Office of Road Inquiry for the first two months, prepared in December for the Annual Report of the Department, shows encouraging results from these inquiries.

"The responses of the Governors and Secretaries of State have been most hearty and cordial, giving evidence of the warmest interest in the work and promises of all the assistance in their power.

"Many members of Congress have responded in like manner. The State geologists are beginning to supply the information asked for of them. Fifty railroads have already sent in reports of their engineers or other officers, many of them very complete and satisfactory. This information is being tabulated, and when it is all received, with that of the geologists, I shall be enabled to make a map showing the location and cost of the best road materials throughout the United States.

"In this work the office of the United States Geological Survey is rendering valuable assistance, and it could be of the greatest service in the general inquiry if its means permitted.

"Nearly all of the Railroad Companies show a willingness to promote the improvement of highways by cheap transportation of materials; and since in any general system of improvement railway transportation will be almost universally required, if the best materials are to be used, this is one of the most encouraging features of the situation.

"*Recent State Highway Legislation.*

"The first bulletin of this office is now in the hands of the printer, and is composed of a brief of the new road laws of fourteen States, with full extracts of the essential portions of the same, and some recommendations made by influential public bodies but not yet carried into legislation.

"The advance in road legislation proceeds on several distinct lines: —

"1. In the direction of more rigid provisions for carrying out the old systems without radical change in the systems themselves.

"2. More liberal tax levies.

"3. Substitution of money for labor taxes.

"4. Local assessment, according to benefits, for construction of new roads.

"5. Construction by townships, with power to issue bonds.

"6. Construction by counties.

"7. State highway commissions.

"8. Provision for working convicts.

"9. Direct State aid to road-building.

"10. Building of State roads.

"The new Road Law of Tennessee (1891) is an admirable example of the first of these classes. By giving to the County Courts full power and direct control over the whole subject of roads, it should eliminate at once the evil influences of local politics and the easy-going methods that generally prevail. The Court classifies the roads, establishes the districts, and appoints the commissioners; each commissioner divides his district into sections and appoints the overseers. The commissioners have full control of the roads and bridges, and can remove the overseers at pleasure. The Court assesses the road tax, within a limit of eight days' work for each male inhabitant between eighteen and forty-five years of age, and of 25 cents per $100 of property. The overseers may dismiss any man whose work is unsatisfactory and proceed against him by suit, as in case of refusal to work or failure to pay the property tax. Damages in such cases are collectible out of any property, except the homestead, or out of wages.

"The overseer on his part is liable to be sued by any citizen for neglect of duty, and to be fined $20 therefor, and commissioners for the same offence are liable to be indicted and fined $50. Such fines to go to the Road Fund.

"In the direction of increased tax levies, Vermont, New Hampshire, North Dakota, and Oregon are conspicuous, the last-named State allowing the County Courts to levy a special tax of 50 cents on the $100, and $2 per head, for a County Road Fund.

"The abolition of labor taxes is absolute in New Jersey, also in Wisconsin, excepting those towns which specifically vote to retain it, and absolute in those counties of New York whose Boards of Supervisors adopt the County System; and it is optional with all the towns in New York by affirmative vote at town meeting, many having already availed of this privilege.

"Construction on the local assessment plan, extending to a limit of three miles on each side of the line of road, obtains to some extent in Oregon, Indiana, and by special acts, in Ohio. In Oregon the county may assume 50 per cent of the cost, and in Ohio a larger share is usually placed on the county list by the act.

"Construction by townships has been quite extensive, and in Pennsylvania and New Jersey, township bonds have been largely and successfully used.

"The County System, however, is the especial feature of recent legislation, many of the new States having started out with it in some form, and many of the older ones having adopted or seriously considered it. The issue of county bonds is provided for in New York, New Jersey, Indiana, Michigan, and Washington, but in the last two a popular vote is requisite to authorize the issue, and in Indiana the term of payment is limited to five years.

"State highway commissions have been constituted in Massachusetts, Vermont, Pennsylvania, Ohio, Michigan, and possibly in other States; these are generally temporary bodies, charged only to inquire and recommend, but in Massachusetts the commission is permanent and has important duties connected with actual road improvement.

"In the working of convicts on roads, New York is making an experiment near Clinton Prison, with State prisoners, and Tennessee makes all persons confined in county jails or work-houses available for highway labor.

"New Jersey is probably the only State giving direct aid to road-building. Such aid is limited to one-third of the cost of roads built by the counties, and to the sum of $75,000 per annum.

"The Highway Commission of Pennsylvania has reported a bill for State aid to the amount of $1,000,000 per annum, to be distributed among the townships in proportion to the road tax paid by them, on condition that they set aside 25 per cent of their tax for making permanent highways.

"Building of State roads has been practised in some Western States, and Washington is now building a road through the Cascade Mountains, under charge of a special commission.

"The Massachusetts Highway Commission has authority to adopt any road as a State highway, to be constructed and maintained as such if the Legislature make appropriation therefor.

"Co-operative road-building, as provided for in New Jersey, has been very successful, abutting land-owners paying one-tenth of the cost, the State one-third, and the county the remainder. Under this law ten miles of road were built in 1892, twenty-five in 1893, and sixty-four are applied for by land-owners for 1894.

"*New Road Construction.— Reduced Cost.*

"Information on this head is meagre as yet, but enough has been gained to show that new construction is proceeding in many parts of the country, and that, as might be expected, increased knowledge and skill, improved machinery and methods, and extended practical experience, are rapidly lessening the cost of good roads. Mr. E. G. Harrison, C.E., of Asbury Park, N.J., under whose supervision permanent roads have been constructed in that State, says: 'Three or four years ago the cost of road-building was $10,000 per mile. Last year I built roads for $3500 per mile; the stone was brought by rail at a cost of $1 per ton for transportation.' Major M. H. Crump, of Bowling Green, Ky., who has built many miles of the excellent highways in that State, says a good Telford road can be built for $2000 per mile, including grading. J. B. Hunnicutt, Professor of Agriculture in the University of Georgia, states the cost of good hard roads recently built in that State, giving one track of stone and one of earth, at $1200 per mile. H. G. Chapin,

Supervisor of East Bloomfield, Ontario County, N.Y., reports the building in the town of Canandaigua, N.Y., of ten miles of single-track stone road, with an earth track on each side, for $900 per mile, the crushed stone being laid one foot deep and eight feet wide. In this case the township owns a movable crusher and prepares its own material, the neighboring farmers delivering field stones at the crusher for 20 cents per load.

"*Benefits of Road Improvement.*

"Information in this regard is more abundant; I select a few well-authenticated cases.

"Hon. Edward Burrough, President of the State Board of Agriculture of New Jersey, says that on the new stone road from Merchantville to Camden, his teams haul eighty-five to one hundred baskets of potatoes where they formerly hauled only twenty-five. Mr. Burrough says further that 'one of our counties has issued $450,000 of 4 per cent bonds and put down sixty miles of stone roads, averaging sixteen feet wide, and though they pay the taxes to meet the interest on these bonds, their tax rate is now lower than it was before the roads were built.'

"Mr. Chapin, heretofore quoted, says of the Canandaigua roads, that they are as good in March as in July, that they have increased the value of the adjoining farms many times the cost of the roads, and that the cost of keeping them in good repair is much less than that of keeping poor roads in poor repair. Mr. Garfield, speaking at the Michigan Engineers' Convention in 1893, says that in his township, while farms have generally been declining in value, the building of a gravel road four miles in length has increased the value of those adjoining it 25 to 40 per cent, and this is not a free, but a toll road.

"The owner of a large tobacco plantation, some miles from Henderson, Ky., having great difficulty in moving his product to market in that city, organized a company and built a toll road. He estimates the increase in the value of his property at threefold, while the road has paid annually over 10 per cent in dividends."

Stone Road, Canandaigua, N. Y., built in April, 1892, no repairs since; was rolled three times in summer of 1892; picture taken March 19, 1894, road built by Ira P. Cribb, Commissioner of Highways.

CHAPTER III.

THE NEW ROADS OF CANANDAIGUA, N.Y.

The people of Canandaigua "builded better than they knew," when they resolved that the way to build roads was to build them, and commenced the construction of what are becoming famous as the cheapest good roads in the country. They builded for all the people of the United States, and opened wide the door of hope for better roads everywhere. They did not wait for legislation nor outside help, but plunged into the work with energy, zeal, and discretion, and the results are, to say the least, remarkable. A neighbor of theirs, the supervisor of an adjoining town, writes regarding the New York County Road Law, the roads in Canandaigua, and the lessons taught by these roads, as follows: —

"*The Question of Good Roads.*

"In your issue of November 3d, in an article on 'How to Improve Our Roads,' you say: 'We hope those who are interested in this reform will abandon the advocacy of national roads, of town roads, of county roads, and concentrate their energies in favor of the

State road plan.' There are in Ontario County a great many friends of the County Road Law, and we regret very much that a paper so highly esteemed, and so largely circulated in the county as the *Post Express*, should disparage the adoption of that system and advocate another, the adoption of which seems to be impossible. The State Road Bill (or Richardson Bill) advocated by Governor Hill was defeated in the Legislature within a few years, and the same influence which defeated it then would, in all probability, defeat it again.

"The County Road Law has passed the Legislature and only awaits adoption by the boards of supervisors to become operative in the several counties. Let us see how it would work in Ontario County; for what can be done in this county can be done in any county in the State.

"Within the last thirty years there have been expended on the highways in this county over $1200 per mile, and, with the exception of a few miles in the town of Canandaigua, they are no better than they were at the beginning of that period; and, should the same system be continued for the next thirty years, a like sum would have been expended and the condition of the highways would be just about the same as it is now. The few miles referred to in Canandaigua are crushed stone (or macadam) roads, built at an expense to the town outside of the regular highway tax. Four or five years ago the town bought a stone-crusher and has expended the $2000 per year allowed by law, under the direction of their very efficient highway commissioners, in building macadam roads, consisting of a crushed stone road-bed about eight feet wide and nearly a foot deep in the centre of a turnpike some twenty-five feet to thirty feet wide, sloping enough to shed the surface water, but not too steep to drive on any part of it, at an expense of $400 to $700 per mile (the smaller sum in cases where the stone has been contributed and drawn into piles by the neighboring farmers without expense to the town). As a result, they have in that town ten miles or more of such roads, and so well pleased are they with the improvement, that they have had a special act passed by the Legislature, during the last session, empowering the town to vote upon the question of expending $2000 per year in addition to the $2000 already allowed by law, in building such roads. Those roads are just as good in December or March as they are in July or September; they have increased the value of the adjoining farms many times the cost of the roads, and the subsequent cost of keeping them in good repair will be much less than the cost (under the ordinary system) of keeping poor roads in poor repair.

"Now suppose our supervisors should adopt the County Road Law and select one hundred miles of highway to be built and maintained by the county, for which the money is to be raised by the sale of bonds running not less than twenty years and drawing not more than 5 per cent interest. These roads must be selected outside of incorporated villages, and as the incorporated villages in this county pay 29½ per cent of all county taxes, the farming community will receive nearly all the benefit and pay only about seven-tenths of the cost; but the villages do not object, for they think (and rightly, too) that access to the villages will be made easier and better.

"But the best feature of the law is that, by its adoption, the highway taxes become payable in money instead of labor, thus doing away at once with the miserable old system under which much of the expenditure has been worse than wasted, and compelling the man who has been in the habit of leaning on a hoe and gossiping with his neighbors, to pay just as good a dollar as the one who has tried to do an honest day's work on the road. As soon as the law is adopted, each town can buy a stone-crusher, and have its commissioners of highways (using the county roads as models, if they choose) expend the tax, in the same amount that is now assessed, in building crushed stone roads, and thus all of the roads in this county can be macadamized in fifteen years. The cost for the first fifteen years, including cost of crushers and rollers, and interest on the bonds, would be about 18 per cent greater than it is now; but, once constructed, the cost of maintaining such a system would be much less, so that at the end of thirty years the county would be money ahead, the bonds would have been paid, and the total expense to the county and to the several towns would have been $1,000,000, while under the present system the cost of keeping roads (passable for three or four months in each year, and full of ruts or mire during the balance of the time) for thirty years, at the present rate of expenditure would have been $1,200,000. After that time one-half the sum now expended would maintain the macadam roads in perfect repair. I need not occupy your space in giving all the computations which have led up to these results, for any of your readers can take pencil and paper and make the computations himself.

"Of late years we have heard a great deal of complaint among producers in regard to the excessive cost of transportation. The produce shipped from this (East Bloomfield) station is transported by railroad, on an average of about five hundred miles to the consumers; and it is transported by wagon roads on an average of three miles from the farms to the station. With the present roads it costs the farmers one-half as much to haul this produce the three miles as they pay the railroads to haul it five hundred miles. With a system of macadam roads the cost of this short haul would be reduced 50 per cent, thus reducing the whole cost of transportation from the farm to the consumer by one-sixth, which would be a saving to the farmers of an amount each year equal to the interest on from $10 to $30 an acre, according to the crop raised (the larger sum being the saving on the potato crop, which is one of the main crops here), and would increase the value of the land (either to hold or to sell) by a like amount. These figures may seem startling, but they are none the less correct.

"We agree with you that a system of State roads,

under which the cities would pay three-fourths of the cost of the country roads, is desirable; but, strange as it may seem, the farmers defeated the Richardson Bill, and would no doubt do so again should the cities give them another opportunity; so that there is very little prospect of ever accomplishing anything by advocating such a system, while there is a law already enacted (the County Road Law) which we can adopt, and which is well suited to accomplish its purpose, the best law, we think, of the eleven passed by as many different State Legislatures during the last two or three years, and all having the same object,—the permanent improvement of the country roads. We hope, then, that you will abandon the advocacy of the State road plan, and use the influence of your valued paper in urging the boards of supervisors to adopt the County Road Law.

"HARRY G. CHAPIN.

"East Bloomfield Station, N.Y., Nov. 6, 1893."

The writer of this book, after a visit to the spot and a careful investigation, is able to confirm all that Supervisor Chapin says of the Canandaigua roads, except that a more careful computation of the cost in detail, including interest and depreciation on machinery, and full pay for volunteer labor and superintendence, would bring the total for the best of them up to about $900 per mile. The visit to these roads, being timed in the midst of a winter thaw, gave an excellent opportunity to test the merits of their construction; they were found so good that farmers were hauling two tons of hay

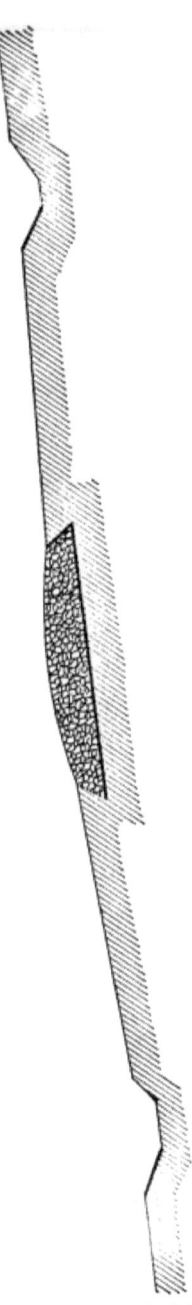

CANANDAIGUA ROADS

with two horses over them, when other roads near by required two horses to a buggy.

The total distance built is about fourteen miles, of which a part is of sufficient width to allow a dirt track on each side of the stone, and part has only the stone track, with a shoulder of earth four or five feet wide on each side. The difference in cost is not great, being only in the grading and culverts; the farmers seem entirely satisfied with the narrower roads. The following are items of cost, etc., given by the Highway Commissioner in charge, Mr. Ira P. Cribb: —

"Built in 1891, in the village of Canandaigua, west part of Bristol Street, 64 rods of road, graded 36 feet wide, macadamized 9 feet wide in the middle, and 9 inches deep, except in a low wet place 20 rods long, where it was made 18 inches deep; all broken stone, not screened nor assorted; no roller used; crushing cost 18 cents per cubic yard, not including interest or use of crusher; average haul from crusher, one mile; three and sometimes four teams used in hauling; three men placed the stone; wages $1.50 for men, $3 for team and man; average total cost, $2.68 per rod.

"Lake Shore road, one mile cost $447, nearly all the stone delivered free, and some labor volunteered (about $100).

"Bristol road, three miles, graded 32 feet wide, macadamized 9 feet wide at top and 10 feet at bottom; 100 rods of it is 18 inches deep, balance about 1 foot; average cost $850 per mile; other roads about the same.

"In some cases the Commissioners pay 20 cents per

cubic yard for the stone delivered at the crusher, in other cases they break up boulders in the fields, at a cost of 30 cents per cubic yard, and the farmers haul them free of charge, in order to clear their fields.

"It is the general opinion that these roads have added $20 or more, per acre, to the value of adjoining lands; the average loads hauled throughout the year are fully doubled."

Mud Road at end of Stone Road, Canandaigua, N. Y., taken March 19, 1894.

CHAPTER IV.

MODERN KENTUCKY ROAD-BUILDING.

The State of Kentucky was famous for its fine roads a generation ago, before many of the Eastern States had made any serious attempt at the improvement of their highways. It is fair to presume, therefore, that Kentucky knows what good roads are, and that her recent road-building is fully abreast if not ahead of the times, — and certainly that the standard of excellence in construction has not been lowered. In this view the following details of a portion of the work lately done there are important and interesting. They show a thoroughness of design and an economy of execution which are instructive to road-builders everywhere.

These details are furnished by Major M. H. Crump, C.E., who has superintended the construction of $200,000 worth of Telford and gravel roads in that State in the last ten years. Major Crump says: "Many miles of 18-foot stone roads have cost less than $2000 per mile, and many miles of 16-foot road have cost less than $1600 per mile. They are built of good limestone, generally found within a mile of the road. These stone roads were constructed by county aid, $1000 being allowed on each completed mile, when not less than three miles were assured. Bonds running thirty years at 5 per cent were sold at par and all taken by citizens of the county. Warren County expended $60,000 in this way, and the county levy has been decreased every year since the roads were built."

The specifications for construction are as follows:—

"*For an* 18-*Foot Roadway.*

"Excavation must be 24 feet wide. Embankment the same.

"Road-bed is graded carefully with a crown of 4 inches.

"Paving consists of selected stone not more than 6 inches long, 4 inches wide, and 9 inches high, which are carefully set by hand, large end on ground. The stone are carefully broken down with long-handled light hammers to a uniform surface and thickness of 8 inches, this surface still to retain a rise or crown of 4 inches. Headers, as the outside courses of stone are called, must be set with great care, so as to bind and hold the pavement together.

"Metal. — On this paving an average thickness of 4 inches of metal broken so as to pass through a $2\frac{1}{2}$ inch ring, and so spread as to be 6 inches in the centre and gradually thin to 2 inches at the headers.

"Clay. — On this metal may be spread one or two inches of clay, to act as a binding material. This is essential on country roads, when a roller is not used and the travel is light.

"Embankments.—In all cases there must be at least 3 feet of earth outside of the line of headers, which must be carefully packed so as to retain the headers in place till they become firmly set.

"Excavations.—Not less than 3 feet outside of headers, and occasionally more space is required for drainage ditches.

"The same specifications apply to 16-foot roadways, which are the principal widths used in this section. The all-important matter is proper shape to the road-bed, so as to produce the proper drainage, the careful setting of headers, and sufficient backing to retain them in place.

"The crown for 16-foot roadway may be made 3 inches, but my experience has always been that 4 inches is better, since on country roads almost the entire traffic occurs on the centre.

"Grading and shaping the road-bed costs from $200 to $500 per mile. The average cost of an 18-foot road, including grading, has been $2200 per mile. Some miles have been constructed for $1800, and some for $2500 per mile."

CHAPTER V.

CONNECTICUT ROADS.

A QUESTION still open to discussion, and one which interests all localities where field stones or quarry spawls are abundant, is whether it is important to crush all the stones that are put into the road.

At the meeting of the Connecticut Board of Agriculture in 1893, Mr. Perry of Worcester said: "From my standpoint I think it is wholly unnecessary to crush all the stones. As far as my experience is concerned, and I have had some experience, two-thirds or three-quarters of the stones that are put in a macadamized road are just as good, if not better, before they are crushed as afterwards, which makes a wonderful difference in the cost of a road. It costs a great deal to carry stone to the stone-crusher, crush it, and then carry this stone back from one to five miles. Supposing you want to improve a highway and want to macadamize it, I would say, put that road into shape, open it out. In our section we have lots of stone. The farmers want to get rid of the stone. One man has said here to-day that he put 168 loads of stone directly into the roads where they were wanted in order to get rid of them. You can readily see that it costs but very little to build macadamized roads if you build them without crushing more than one-quarter of the material. I do not think, on the average, it would cost more than one-half as much, and when you have done it, you have got just as good a road as if you had crushed all the stone.

"My idea of macadamized road is that it ought not to cost more than from $1000 to $2000 dollars per mile. When you put $5000 into a mile of road you have got too much money there, and too little somewhere else. On all your farms around here you have got hundreds of thousands of loads of stone. Some of them you want to get rid of. When you have a load of stone of any shape, bring that stone on to the road that you want to macadamize, let somebody be there to look after and take care of it, and then when you have got your stone in in good shape, put a few crushed stone on top; and if you put on good gravel, and perhaps a little clay to make it heavy, I will guarantee that you will have as good a road as can be made with all crushed stone, and at not more than half the cost." (Applause.)

Mr. Kirkman said: "I was very glad to hear Mr. Perry tell us how a good road should be made. I live in a small town, with a grand list of half a million. Our tax is about $5000 a year, and we appropriate $3000 of that for our roads. We build from half a mile to a mile of macadamized road every year, and have done it for the last fifteen years. We join the city of Hartford, and our roads are better than the roads in the outskirts of the city. Our roads have cost less than $1000 a mile.

We have a range of trap rock 300 feet high that is accessible, and the stones are put at the bottom as large as they can be thrown into the cart; smaller stones are put on top, and then gravel on top of those, and we slope the road, if it is 25 feet wide, $2\frac{1}{2}$ feet on each side; so that our own roads are made very economically. Farmers do the work and take the pay."

Mr. Augur. "I would like to ask Mr. Perry the depth of the crushed stone that he puts on."

Mr. Perry. "I say I should not think it necessary to have more than three or four inches of crushed stone."

Mr. Augur. "The distinct difference between a Telford road and a macadam road is that Macadam's theory was that the stone should all be crushed to nearly a uniform size, and for the reason that when stones are put on a road to the thickness of about ten inches, the larger stones will have a tendency to work up all the time to the surface, just as, if you shake a pan of gravel, you will find the larger stones on the top. That is a tendency we shall have to admit. Telford's theory was that larger stones could be used for the bottom. His system was to make a sort of pavement, setting the stones with some care, and then applying a thinner layer than Macadam would have recommended, of crushed stone. Telford argued that the bottom course of cheaper stone was really the foundation for the road proper, which was of the crushed stone. I think that Mr. Perry conveyed the idea that a very thin layer of crushed stone is necessary. Now, my observation is, that it is not wise to lay too thin a layer of crushed stone upon the surface of other stone underneath, and for this reason, that you need to get more than one or two stones on top of each other. If you are going to make a permanent surface of crushed stone, put on enough to pack together; otherwise you will have the crushed stone working loose constantly, which is a source of trouble in a road, and your surface will be gone just at the time it ought to be in its best condition."

Here we have both sides of the question fairly presented, and by their ancient champions as well as by their modern. Fortunately, it would seem now to be only a question of ascertainable facts, "a condition, not a theory that confronts us"; for if on these Connecticut roads, built in this manner and tested for years, the large stones do *not* "work up to the surface" under the stress of that frosty climate, and the thin crushed stone or gravel surfacing does *not* "work loose" under the wheels, then that form of construction may safely be adopted elsewhere, and will be a great saving in cost in many localities. The Canandaigua road-builders, for instance, might by this means save $200, or more, per mile, on the present low cost of their roads, and put more stone in them than they do now.

Where roads are constructed with tile or other subdrainage, or on a thoroughly porous subsoil, and the action of frost practically eliminated, it would seem to be a thoroughly safe method to put a good proportion of the stones in the bottom without crushing.

CHAPTER VI.

CHEAP STONE ROADS IN VIRGINIA, MICHIGAN, NEW JERSEY, AND MARYLAND.

THE low-priced hard roads in New York, Connecticut, and Kentucky, heretofore described, are all located where the material was close at hand, abundant, and cheap; but there are some instances of good roads built at low cost under the opposite conditions.

In Alexandria County, Va., a portion of the old mail road from the Washington and Ohio Junction northward, lately rebuilt, was covered with 4 inches of hand broken stone, 9 feet wide, and overlaid with 6 inches of gravel, at a cost of $1139 per mile. In this case the stone was gathered with some difficulty, and the county paid $1.50 per cubic yard for it in place and broken; the contractor paid 25 cents per yard for breaking it by hand on the road-bed. The road was well rolled and stands well under a heavy travel.

Alexandria County levies a tax of 50 cents per $100 for road purposes, and this road was built out of the proceeds of such tax.

The experience of Bay County, Mich., carries some

Country Road, built by Frank Hume, Chairman of the Board of Supervisors, of Alex. Co., Va.; cost $1,100 per mile; six inches of broken stone, four inches of bank gravel; has worn well. Chas. Schaff, Artist.

valuable lessons. It was related by Mr. H. C. Thompson, at the Engineers' Convention, as follows: —

"*Stone Roads in Bay County.*

"In 1880, the board of supervisors conceived the idea that the highways should be improved permanently, and set themselves at work to formulate a plan for so doing. A proposition to raise $100,000 on the bonds of the county was submitted to a vote of the people, and was carried. Committees were appointed by the board of supervisors to visit localities where permanent roads had been constructed, and work was begun on several of the main thoroughfares.

"There being no suitable material in the county for constructing the roads, stone was procured in Ohio, and conveyed by boats to the Saginaw River, where it was placed on docks and drawn by teams to the respective roads.

"The Ohio stone not proving satisfactory, — being too soft, — a better quality was obtained on the shore of Lake Huron, at Bay Port, where it was loaded on cars and conveyed by rail to its destination. Considerable gravel was used in the construction of the roads at different times, and this was procured from gravel beds near Mason. All the material used had to be imported, thus making the cost considerable; but the result of having good roads at all times of the year is shown in there being a uniform price and market for all farm products, and never at any time is there a scarcity of any of the necessaries of life, on account of bad roads.

"The soil is a sandy loam, and the surface practically level, rising about three feet to a mile from the level of the bay, which affords sufficient grade to convey surface water through artificial channels. The first object to be sought was drainage, and this was accomplished by constructing suitable drains on both sides of the grade. An excavation twelve feet wide and about one foot deep was then made on one side of the grade to receive the first layer of stone, which was composed of the larger stones, laid flat with edges close together. This foundation would average four inches in thickness. Upon this layer were placed stones of smaller size, and in the early part of the work the surface was made smooth by pounding with hammers, until the stones on the surface would be about one and a half inches in diameter. Later, the top dressing was put on entirely with crushed stone. Gravel was also used as a top dressing, but this was so easily displaced that the crushed stone was adopted. There was no roller used in compacting the stone or the sub-grade. On this account a great many of the stones would be displaced by the traffic, and it would require some time before a uniform surface would be made, and this not until the ruts made by the wheels had been filled by raking in the loose material. A road machine or scraper has been used to do this work, with good results. The first few years the practice was to make the width of stone twelve feet, but later nine feet was adopted, with a margin of two feet of earth on one side and eleven on the opposite, making a road-bed twenty-two feet wide.

CHEAP STONE ROADS.   53

"This has proven to be of sufficient width for all purposes. The surface of the road has a crown of one foot, and the stone work has a crown of four inches which soon wears down to level, and after about three years' use, requires a top dressing of fine broken stone, to fill up uneven places. The depth of material laid loose was twelve inches, but when compacted would not be more than eight inches. The stone costs, delivered on the railroad, about $5.80 per cord, which would lay about three rods in length. The earth work, hauling, and laying the stone was let by contract to the lowest bidders, and varied from $1.60 per rod where the material did not have to be hauled more than one-half mile, to $5.50 per rod where the distance was five miles.

"The act authorizing the issue of bonds also provides that a sum not exceeding two mills each year could be spread upon the cities and townships, including the stone road district, and the money thus raised, about $30,000 annually, could be used in extending and repairing the roads, which has been done each year, until there are at present about fifty miles in good condition.

"The cities have paid about nine-tenths of the whole amount expended. The average cost has been about $6 per rod."

Returning to cases where the material is close at hand, we have another cheap road in Hopewell, Mercer County, N.J.

In this case small field stones were delivered in the road-bed, and the top ones broken by hand, for 35 cents per ton; this was covered with screenings from a stone-crusher and made an excellent road, at a cost for single track of about $1000 per mile.

Professor Miller, Director of the Maryland Agricultural Experiment Section, at the late meeting of the State Road League in Baltimore, gave an instance of the improvement of a bit of very bad road by the co-operation of the road supervisor and the neighboring farmers, through whose efforts a half-mile of excellent stone pike had been built for $200.

To face p. 56.

CHAPTER VII.

INEFFECTIVE COUNTY ROAD LAWS. — THE LOCAL OPTION LAW OF NEW JERSEY.

VERY high hopes were entertained by the friends of road improvement in New York, of immediate good results to flow from the optional County Road Law, enacted in that State last winter through the persistent effort of Governor Flower and others; but these hopes have faded steadily as board after board of supervisors has rejected the law, on the ground of its being unsatisfactory to their several constituencies. In Missouri the same state of things prevails, and nearly the same in Michigan, where only two or three counties have accepted the law, although the constitution of the State was amended expressly to admit its passage.

All this seems to indicate that legislation in this direction has gone beyond the education of the mass of voters, and that a new line of advance must be secured. Under these circumstances we turn naturally to those various other methods of improvement which have been more successfully introduced and are in actual and effective practice. Among these none is so conspicuous as the New Jersey Local Option and Co-operation

Plan briefly described in Chapter II. This plan in detail is as follows: —

The law provides that "whenever there shall be presented to the board of chosen freeholders of any county a petition signed by the owners of at least two-thirds of the lands and real estate fronting or bordering on any public road or section of road in such county, not being less than one mile in length, praying the board to cause such road or section to be improved under this act, and setting forth that they are willing that the peculiar benefits conferred on the lands fronting or bordering on said road or section shall be assessed thereon, in proportion to the benefits conferred, to an amount not exceeding 10 per centum of the entire cost of the improvement. it shall be the duty of the board to cause such improvements to be made; *provided*, that the estimated cost of all improvements made under this act in any county in any one year shall not exceed one-half of 1 per centum of the ratables of such county for the last preceding year.

"4. *And be it enacted*, that one-third of the cost of all roads constructed in this State under this act shall be paid for out of the State Treasury; *provided*, that the amount so paid shall not in any one year exceed the sum of $75,000; if one-third of said cost shall exceed said sum, the said $75,000 shall be apportioned by the Governor and the President of the State Board of Agriculture amongst the counties of the State in proportion to the cost of roads constructed therein for such year, as shown by the statements of costs filed in the office of the President of the State Board of Agriculture."

Under this law, as before stated, 10 miles of road were built in 1892, 25 miles in 1893, and over 60 miles are laid out for the current year.

This is a satisfactory rate of increase, and shows that this system has met the wants of the people of New Jersey in a remarkable degree.

It has the merit that it offers a local initiative, and does not require the education of a whole county to start the work; while the object lessons with which it is filling the State are fast completing the general education of the people on the road question.

It gives the opportunity for any community of enterprising citizens, or for those having especially bad roads or especial need of good ones, to help themselves without delay, and to have the help of the county and State as well.

It "helps those who help themselves," in a practical fashion; and no locality can be jealous of the help so given to others, since the same help is offered to all.

The authors of this law are justly proud of its success, and proud of the fact that their State is the first to give direct aid to road-building through any co-operative plan.

If it shall prove that general county road-building is in advance of public sentiment, it would seem wise for other States to avail themselves of the experience of New Jersey, whereby, instead of awaiting the slow process of education alone, they can have education and road-building going on together, hand in hand, and with constantly augmented speed and power; for in every State, and probably in every county, some neighborhoods will be found with enterprise and courage enough to take prompt advantage of such an opportunity.

This plan can no longer be regarded as an experiment, since its success has been so pronounced; still, it may be entered upon on ever so small a scale and its application expanded by degrees, as its merits are shown, in each State. It requires no costly State organization, but may be committed at first, as it is in New Jersey, to the State Board of Agriculture, or to some other existing organization.

CHAPTER VIII.

PROPOSED AMENDMENTS TO THE NEW JERSEY ROAD LAW.

The State Aid Law of New Jersey has been so successful in practice that any suggestions of improvement in that law, made by those concerned in its administration, are of especial importance.

At the recent meeting of the State Road Association at Trenton, the President, Hon. Edward Burrough, who, as Chairman of the State Board of Agriculture, has charge of the execution of the present law, made the following recommendations for its amendment:—

"1. Amend Section 1: Making it obligatory for the engineer to file a copy of the specifications and a diagram of the road with the President of the State Board of Agriculture (or the State officer who executes the functions now performed by him).

"2. Amend Section 2: (*a*) Requiring the supervisor to be selected from among the signers of the petition or a judicious freeholder residing in the taxing district, or in one of the townships through which the road runs.

"(*b*) Reduce the pay of supervisor from $5 to $3 per day.

"(c) Compel the townships to do the grading, according to lines approved by engineer and State officer as their contribution.

"(d) Contractor to keep the road in repair for one year after the acceptance of the same by Board of Freeholders, and 5 per cent of the cost to be and remain in county treasury until the expiration of the yearly limit (this can be provided in the contracts now).

"3. The duty now performed by the President of the State Board of Agriculture to be placed on a State officer known as Commissioner of Roads, who shall have an office in the State Capitol, and be furnished with office supplies, maps, etc., and who shall be considered in all respects a State officer, and supplied with railroad passes, and have his actual travelling expenses when on duty for the State paid, and who shall have a stipulated salary in lieu of all fees or other compensation of any kind.

"4. Increase the annual State appropriation to at least $150,000, and the percentage of State aid to (say) 50 per cent. Should the State do this, it might be well to amend Section 7 so as to reduce the amount authorized by a county to be spent, to one-third of 1 per cent of the ratables."

After much discussion, mainly on the subject of extending the State aid to the construction of gravel and shell roads as well as of stone roads, the Association finally agreed to recommend the following amendments to the Road Law: —

"First. That the amount to be appropriated by the county in any one year for road-building and repairs shall not exceed one-fourth of 1 per cent on the ratables of said county.

"Second. That the State shall pay 40 per cent, the townships 25 per cent, the adjacent taxpayers 10 per cent, and the county the balance.

"Third. That after the word 'stone' in the section describing the material of the road-bed, be inserted the words 'oyster shells, gravel, or iron bog ore.'

"Fourth. That the Board of Freeholders shall select from the roads petitioned for the ones to be built, they having in mind the most used ones and the distributing of the benefits to all parts of the county.

"Fifth. That the President of the State Board shall not approve of more roads in one year than the State appropriation will pay its 40 per cent of the building, nor the Board of Freeholders put under contract in any one year more than the year's appropriation will pay

CHAPTER IX.

FURTHER MODIFICATION OF THE SAME LAW SUGGESTED.

The special feature of this law, aside from the State aid of one-third, is the giving to the property-holders along any section of road the right to demand the improvement of their road upon their agreeing to bear one-tenth of the cost of the work.

In some of the Western States roads are built by assessing a part of the cost on a strip of one, two, or three miles wide on each side of the road, and the part of the cost so assessed is generally much more than one-tenth. But neither of these plans is quite just. In the one case, the property-holders fronting on the road may be very little more benefited than those behind them, who use it quite as much as the abutters, while they pay no more than distant citizens of the county; in the Western method, a strip of any given width might take in farms that were not benefited, or leave out others that were. In fact, the benefits will rarely, if ever, follow parallel lines. Roads that are important enough to require systematic reconstruction will generally be such as radiate from railway stations or boat

Church Road, Camden County, New Jersey. Weight of Two-horse Load, 7,922 pounds; weight of Wagon 2,300 pounds. Telford Road, built by State Aid, 1893.

landings, market towns, county seats, or villages, and the district benefited by each will widen rapidly as the distance from the common centre increases. Taking the case of four main roads diverging from a railway station, at right angles to each other, these roads at a distance of five miles will be seven miles apart, and the benefit district of each will be a triangle with its apex at the station and a width of seven miles at the base. The bounds of the district, moreover, will be modified by many such natural obstacles as streams, swamps, hills, valleys, etc., which will divert travel to or from a particular road, or by artificial conditions, like the location of factories, creameries, grain elevators, schools, or churches. All these conditions, however, are susceptible of a fairly exact determination, and the benefit district of a road can be almost as accurately defined as the drainage area of a stream. When it is so defined, such a district forms an ideal unit of action for road improvement; the interests of all its people are identical though unequal, and the share of expense each ought to bear can be safely left to the commissioners charged with its assessment, with an appeal to the courts, as it is done under the New Jersey law; so that nothing should prevent the harmonious action of the inhabitants of the district, and there need be no fear of unequal or undue burdens being imposed on any one of them, the only question to settle being whether, as a body, they can afford to be assessed for their share of the cost of the road.

Just what should be the share of those "peculiarly

benefited," or, in other words, of the "habitual users" of a certain section of road, is open to much discussion. At first glance it would seem proper that it should be a large one; but when we consider that the same people must ultimately, through their county and State taxes, help to pay for all the roads in the State, a very moderate share would seem sufficient; and if this plan is to be relied upon to produce object lessons for the whole State, it must be made attractive enough to secure its prompt acceptance by many localities. The benefit district would include, of course, much more territory than the abutting farms and should therefore pay more than one-tenth, if that is the just share of such farms; if it paid one-sixth, and the State one-third, the county would have to pay only an even half.

The Local Option Law does not supersede the County Road Law in New Jersey, and should not in any other State. It fills a gap until the County System can be established by the acceptance of the people; it applies more especially to the distinctly rural regions. Counties which are largely suburban, or which contain large cities, can see more direct advantages in the building of good roads through immediate rise in value of lots and lands, and will be more ready to incur the necessary expense or debt than those situated at a distance from the centres of population and dependent wholly upon agriculture.

Following the New Jersey law in general plan, a Benefit District Act would take something of the following form:—

1. Whenever there shall be presented to the Board of Supervisors of any county in the State, a petition signed by the owners of not less than one-half of the lands fronting or bordering on any section of road already established, or proposed to be established, in such county, asking for a survey and estimate of the cost of building or rebuilding such road in a substantial and permanent manner, it shall be the duty of said Board to cause such survey and estimate to be made and suitably published for the information of the petitioners.

2. Whenever, thereafter, the petitioner shall file with the Board of Supervisors a map or description of the lands which will, in their opinion, be peculiarly benefited by the construction or improvement of such road, together with the written consent and request of the owners of three-fifths of such lands, that all the lands so benefited, together with the personal property in the same district, shall be assessed in proportion to the benefits conferred, for the cost of such construction or improvement, to the amount of one-sixth of the total cost thereof, payable in six annual instalments, it shall be the duty of the said Board of Supervisors to cause such road to be constructed or improved in the manner provided by the County Road Law for the construction of county roads, whether said Board has or has not adopted the general county system under said law.

3. The said Board of Supervisors shall assess upon any township in which said road shall lie, one-sixth of the cost of the portion thereof lying in said township, and shall pay one-third of the total cost out of the county treasury.

4. The remaining one-third of the cost of all such roads shall be paid out of the State treasury upon the certificate of the State Engineer that the road has been properly constructed and that he has furnished the specifications therefor, and has properly supervised the construction thereof; and for this purpose he is authorized to appoint an inspector to be paid out of the State treasury, at the rate of four dollars per day.

5. All roads built under the provisions of this act shall be held to be county roads, and shall be kept permanently in repair by the county.

6. The assessment of one-sixth upon the township shall be spread over a term of — years, or the township may issue and sell bonds for its prompt payment.

7. The county may issue and sell its bonds for the purposes of this act, as provided by the County Road Law for the building of county roads.

Upon the basis suggested, the cost to the inhabitants of the benefit district would not be onerous compared with the benefits conferred, nor even when compared with the customary taxation for road purposes.

Supposing the district to average two miles in width, there would be an area of two square miles, or 1280 acres of land, to bear the one-sixth part of the cost of each mile of road. If we should double the cost of the Canandaigua roads heretofore mentioned, as a safe estimate for average country roads, we should have $1800 per mile. One-sixth of this would be $300, or 24 cents per acre; or, if paid in six years, 4 cents per acre annually. This is supposing the whole amount to be

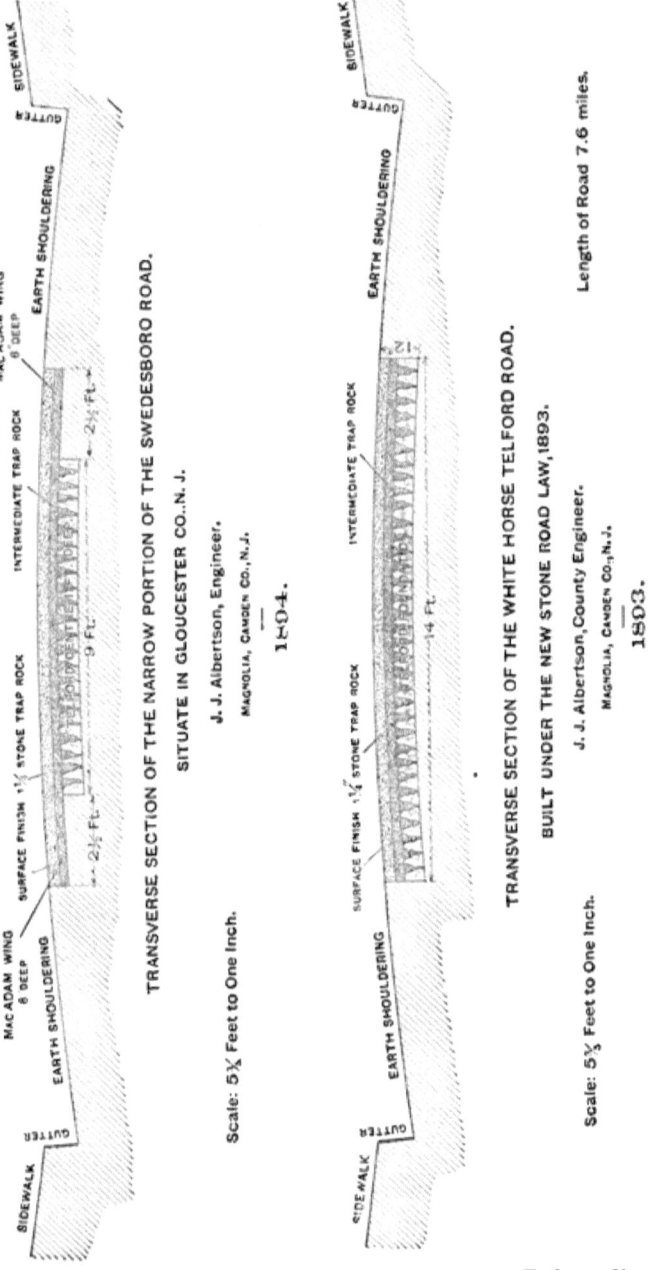

To face p. 66.

assessed on farming lands and the usual personal property of farmers. If there were villages, factories, mills, or banks, on the line of road, or persons paying taxes on any considerable amounts of personal estate, the amount per acre would be lightened accordingly.

The justice of including personal property in this assessment can hardly be questioned when the same is done by the county and State in respect to the other five-sixths of the cost of the road.

The amount paid by the inhabitants of the district in the period of six years would be trifling compared with the advantages of the improvement to them during that time; the future advantages would be clear gain. Another gain would be in the reduced cost of maintenance of a good road, as compared with a bad one. The average expenditure on country roads is probably $30 per mile per year; the few stone roads in this country have drawn so much travel from other roads that the cost of repairs on them is above a proper allowance. In some cases, however, it is given as low as $10 per mile yearly, and on purely country roads should not exceed $20 per mile for many years.

The New Jersey law makes all roads built on the co-operative plan, county roads, and provides that they are to be maintained at the county cost forever. This arrangement would enable the benefit district to put all its ordinary road tax on the improvement of branch roads tributary to the improved road, and gradually bring these roads up to an equally good condition.

The average annual road tax is about 10 cents per acre, and the increase of 4 cents would not be seriously felt, but it might be judicious to exempt the benefit district from a part of the ordinary road taxes during the six years period, and place a much higher share of the improvement tax upon it.

Church Road Camden Co., N. J., before macadamizing; four mules to half a load

To face p. 68.

CHAPTER X.

STATE AID AND THE METHOD OF GIVING IT.

One chief advantage in giving State aid to road construction is that the city population of the State is thereby enabled to contribute something toward its due proportion of the needed outlay: we may say enabled rather than compelled, since a willingness to do this has been in many cases especially conspicuous.

Inhabitants of cities find their own interests subserved by the improvement of country roads, in many ways; indeed, the tax levied by bad roads is a more direct money tax upon them than upon the rural population. The farmer, in the season of mud, can stay at home and live on what he has raised, and when he is driven by necessity or tempted by high prices to drag some of his produce to market, unless he hires the hauling done he does not pay the mud tax in hard cash, and often does not feel it, while the city dweller cannot live without his daily supplies from the farm, and must pay daily and in money the larger share of all extra cost attending their transportation, wherever and howsoever it may have been incurred.

In Springfield, Ill., a few years ago, during a long

period of wet weather in the early spring, the price of hay went up to $30 per ton, and the market was supplied by railroad from outside of the State, while on farms a few miles from the city, hay was plenty at $10 per ton, but embargoed by mud. In this case the mud tax could not have been more direct if it had been levied on every horse and cow in that city, and if so levied, the rate would probably not have been less than $20 per head on all such animals. The farmer lost a market, but the townsman lost money in hand. Instances of this sort could be multiplied indefinitely. Again, all the active business of cities, whether commercial or productive, would clearly be promoted by the improvement of country roads, through the cheapening of the distribution of goods and collection of raw materials, while the yearly increasing sojourn of city residents in country districts gives them a very direct interest in the condition of the highways and byways therein.

Taking for granted, then, the willingness of the cities to contribute their share, and assuming the recent action of various legislatures as indicating a general disposition toward State aid in some form, the question as to what shape such aid should take becomes pertinent and important.

Massachusetts boldly proposes the building of State roads wherever its commissioners may approve; New York has twice nearly passed a law appropriating ten millions of dollars for a great system of highways uniting all the county seats in the State, on east and west, and north and south lines; while Washington and Idaho are both building State roads at this moment. New Jersey, on the other hand, gives a local contribution to the pioneers of road-building in any part of the State, and Pennsylvania proposes to follow this example on a vastly larger scale.

The Massachusetts law has the prudent proviso, that while the commission may lay out and establish State roads *ad libitum*, such roads are only to be built when the Legislature makes the required appropriations, and it remains to be seen whether local jealousies will not prevent any practical result from this law. In the New York plan, while local jealousy on a large scale is done away with by the grandeur of the scheme (a sort of universal log-rolling), it is probable that when all the lines were laid out, and it became evident that in some places stretches of practically useless road were to be built to carry out a geographical plan, while a large share of the business centres and actual thoroughfares in the State were neglected, such an opposition would speedily arise as would put an end to the whole scheme and leave the State worse off than before.

The same money spent in building the same length of road in each county, but so located as to radiate from shipping points and other business centres, and to connect towns and villages not joined by railroads, would be of much greater benefit; and how much greater still if it were used to stimulate local effort and contribution, and so induced the expenditure of twice or thrice as much by counties, towns, and neighborhoods, in the same direction!

Ten millions of dollars spent by the State, on the New Jersey basis of one-third State aid, would secure the expenditure of thirty millions, and, at an average of $1500 per mile, the building of 20,000 miles of road, which is about one-fourth of all the roads of the State.

An important branch of State aid, or rather a preliminary to such aid, in States which have not reached the point of helping in actual road construction, consists in providing,—

1. A permanent highway commission.
2. A State engineer for roads, with suitable assistance.
3. A careful survey of the State for road materials.

None of these involve any great outlay compared with the benefits to be expected, nor do they necessarily commit the State to any further action involving such outlay.

A model for the first is found in the Massachusetts law, epitomized in the appendix to this volume, and for the second, in the report and bill of the Maryland Road League.

Regarding the need of a survey of road materials, the Massachusetts commission uses the following language: "To put the road-masters of the State in possession of the knowledge required in their difficult tasks, it will be necessary to make a somewhat careful study of the bed rocks, from the point of view of their fitness for the construction of highways, and to delineate the results on appropriate maps, to be accompanied by the necessary descriptions. The information thus obtained should be so presented that the supervisors of highways in each town may know the relative value of all the resources in the way of construction materials which they can command. The cost of such an examination and description would probably not exceed the expense now incurred in constructing ten miles of ordinary good highway, and the saving which would be effected in any one year would probably repay many fold the expense of the inquiry."

In connection with and supplementary to this survey, the Highway Commission might be charged to negotiate with all railroad companies in the State, and if need be in adjoining States, in order to secure the lowest possible rates of transportation, not only for the best surfacing metal obtainable, but for such inferior materials as would serve for the substructure of roads, where the best qualities of stone would be too costly. On many accounts this service might be the most important the Commission could render. The railroad companies are fully alive to their interest in highway improvement, and many of them are prepared to make great concessions in its aid when approached with the full authority of the State and the assurance of its earnest effort in that direction.

CHAPTER XI.

ANOTHER FORM OF STATE AID. CONVICT LABOR.

THERE are three sides to the question of working convicts on the highways, or rather two sides and a broad middle ground. The negative side is taken by the Prison Association of New York, and by penologists generally, and is defended by the New York society in this language: —

"Touching the proposed law, entitled 'An act to provide for the employment of convict labor on the wagon roads of this State,' the following resolution was unanimously adopted by the executive committee of the Prison Association of New York: —

"'*Resolved*, That this association most emphatically deems the employment of convicts upon the public roads as demoralizing alike to the public and the convicts themselves; and that the corresponding secretary be instructed to reply to the communication of the New York State Board of Trade an expression of the opinion of this association.'

"There were present at the meeting of the executive committee, Messrs. Edward B. Merrill, James McKeen, Lispenard Stewart, Felix Adler, John R. Thomas, Benjamin Ogden Chisolm, Frederick G. Lee, and the corresponding secretary.

"There was a full expression of opinion, and previous utterances of the association on the subject were brought before the meeting. The feeling expressed was —

"1. That such employment of convicts would as seriously interfere with labor outside the prisons as any other form of convict labor.

"2. That the State convicts could only be employed on State roads, unless there was a violation of the law which prohibits the employment of convicts under contracts. If the counties employed them, they would be obliged to make a contract with the State for them.

"3. That a very large body of keepers would be required to prevent escapes; that escapes would frequently occur; and that there would be a constant necessity for shooting convicts in order to prevent their getting away. There would soon be a death rate among our convict population approaching that known to have existed among the convicts of the South who were employed on public works.

"4. In many cases the prejudice against convict labor would require a military force to protect the convicts who were at work.

"5. (*a*) It has been found a hardening and demoralizing process to the convicts themselves to employ them in public places; (*b*) and it has been found by penologists to be a demoralizing process to the public at large to see this daily spectacle of shame.

"These are but a part of the reasons advanced for a

protest from the Prison Association of New York upon the passage of this bill. I am sure that an investigation will show you that this decision is fully in harmony with that of the most advanced penologists, not only of this country, but of the entire world.

"With great respect, I am yours, very sincerely,
"WM. M. F. ROUND,
"*Corresponding Secretary.*
"FRANK S. GARDNER, ESQ.,
"*Secretary New York State Board of Trade,*
55 *Liberty Street, New York.*"

This is a view of the question natural to men whose minds are fixed on the need to society of the reformation of criminals; opposed to it is the opinion of many equally good citizens who seek the public good in other ways, and especially in the direction of improved means of communication, and who see, in the multitude supported in idleness in our jails and prisons as a reward for crime, or employed in prison manufactures to the injury of honest artisans, a labor force sufficient to mend all the roads in the country if it could be so applied, and which they believe could be so applied without prejudice to free labor, since it would be employed on work not now done at all and would therefore not compete with any class of workingmen. The advocates of convict road-work insist further that the outdoor life and exercise afforded by such employment must benefit the health and morals of the prisoners, that the public and visible punishment of criminals would deter others from the commission of crime, and that the labor so supplied would accomplish a great good not attainable by any other means.

They point to the practical working of the system in many places, for instance, at Cranston, R.I., and at Charlotte, N.C.: in the latter place, convicts have built many miles of beautiful roads running out of the city in all directions, and with such satisfaction to the people that the special law under which it was done is now being extended to other counties.

In other Southern States, where the Convict Lease System with all its objectionable features still prevails, it is clear that a transfer of the prisoners from irresponsible and often inhumane private employ to the care of States or counties would be a saving kindness to them, while it would wipe out a public disgrace and benefit the entire community.

Some of the apprehensions of the New York Prison Association do not appear to have been well founded.

The Legislature passed the bill in spite of their protest, and an experiment having been made, in the employment at road-making, of the convicts at Clinton Prison, the results as reported by Warden Thayer "are entirely satisfactory." There was no interference with the convicts by citizens except in two cases where intoxicated men offered them liquor; no apparent demoralizing effects on the prisoners or the public; no shooting of convicts, and only three men attempted to escape. The Warden therefore, in his report on the subject, concludes as follows: "That a limited number of convicts can be worked successfully is now an established fact."

But, on the other hand, when we examine the Warden's financial statement, we find but little, if any, economy in the use of convicts, as compared with the employment of free labor for the same work. The cost of guards and of the search for escaped convicts was equal to 91 cents for each day's labor done, which, considering the comparative efficiency of such labor, is very near its full value, the day's work being only eight hours.

Again, it may be safely predicted that when road-making becomes a great business of the country, the introduction of labor-saving appliances will do away with a large share of the hand labor now requisite in laying a stone or gravel road; the material being generally transported by railroad, will then be transferred to wagons without shovelling, and from the wagons mechanically spread in its place, so that almost nothing will be left for convicts to do on the line of the road.

These considerations strengthen the position of those who hold the middle ground of the question, which is that State prisoners should be employed wholly in the preparation of road materials, and in places where they can be guarded and secluded as easily and cheaply as in the prisons.

The plan proposed for this is in substance as follows: for the State, 1. To buy some of the territory which contains the best rock within its limits.

2. To make the necessary railway connections, hav-

ing first secured the permanent agreement of all its leading railroad companies to carry road materials at the cost of hauling, on condition, if required, of the State furnishing to them a certain amount of track ballast free of charge, or at cost.

3. Having erected the necessary buildings and walls or stockades, and provided the best machinery for quarrying and crushing rock, to bring all able-bodied State Prison convicts and put them at this work.

4. The counties to put their jail prisoners and tramps at the work of grading, draining, and preparing the roads for macadamizing.

5. The State to furnish the broken stone free on board cars, as its contribution to road improvement.

The cost to the State, in addition to the maintenance and guarding of the convicts, would be only that of fuel and oil, explosives, and use of machinery, or, according to the Massachusetts Commission report, $6\frac{8}{10}$ cents per cubic yard of broken stone, amounting, for the 1200 yards required to lay a mile of single track road 9 feet wide and 8 inches deep, to $81.60.

The remaining cost would be the railroad freight, amounting, for an average distance of 100 miles, to not more than 28 cents per yard,* $336; the wagon haul, averaging possibly $2\frac{1}{2}$ miles, 30 cents per yard, $360; and the rolling, superintendence, and incidentals (not including engineering, which would be a general county charge) 10 cents per yard; making the total local cost 68 cents per cubic yard, or $816 per mile.

* See page 86.

The wagon haul is estimated on the basis of the country price of $3 per day for team and driver, and of hauling (over the hard road as it is made) two yards at a load, and an average travel for a team of 25 miles a day.

This plan brings the expense of road improvement so low that no elaborate scheme of taxation, bonding, or borrowing would be necessary, and all its benefits could be speedily and universally realized. The best plan for carrying it out would perhaps be to let the "benefit district," as heretofore defined, pay one-third of the cost, by instalments, and the township one-third; the county to pay the remainder, and to advance the amount for the district, with a rebate or discount to all individuals who preferred to pay in cash, so that no one would be put in debt against his will.

The cost to the district on this basis of division would be $272 per mile. Taking the average width benefited, as in Chapter VII., at 2 miles, or 1280 acres for each mile of road, the total charge per acre would be 21 cents, or 3 cents per acre annually, if spread over seven years.

Road Building in North Carolina. Blowing up Stumps by Dynamite. Opening of Lake Shore Avenue. July 4, 1890.

CHAPTER XII.

WHAT THE RAILROADS WILL DO FOR THE HIGHWAYS.

The deep concern of the railroads of the country in the condition of its highways is universally recognized; it was particularly well expressed at the Michigan Engineers' Convention by Mr. E. W. Muenscher, Chief Engineer of the M. & G. R. Railway, who said: "No interest in the State of Michigan would be more benefited by good roads than the railroads. During a large part of the year much of their rolling-stock is lying idle because farmers cannot bring their produce to the station. At other times they cannot get cars enough to haul away this produce, and the sidings, elevators, and warehouses are gorged to overflowing; extra train forces must be employed; men in other lines of traffic who need cars are denied, and general disturbance of business, delay, and loss follow. Good roads would distribute this business more uniformly over the year, to the mutual advantage of the companies and their patrons, to say nothing of the increase of population, and production and prosperity which would follow."

The same speaker made these excellent practical suggestions. "There is one way in which the railroads might greatly help on and hasten the good work without cost to themselves. If we are ever to have anything better than dirt roads in Michigan, we have got to depend almost entirely on gravel. This material is found in vast quantities in the drift which covers the entire lower peninsula, but the deposits are local, and there are large sections in which a stone as large as a hazel nut would be a curiosity. The cost of hauling gravel by wagon to such localities is so great as to forbid its use. It is here that the railroads could do good work. Most of them pass through or near large gravel beds. If, at times when many of their flat cars are lying idle, they would load them with gravel and deliver it at each station along their lines at bare cost, to be used in building gravel roads each way from those stations, they would greatly diminish this most serious obstacle. Some of them also own their own steam shovels, which at times could be used in loading the cars, with a further saving in cost; and other roads might well afford to purchase these excavators for this purpose."

The disposition of the railway companies themselves to aid in road improvement may be judged by the following extracts from a portion of the letters received by the Road Inquiry office on this subject, from which, and the fact that while some of the other roads are noncommittal, none of them are opposed to giving such aid, it would seem that the companies generally will be ready to do their full share, whenever the opportunity offers to promote road-building on any extended scale.

BIRMINGHAM & ATLANTIC RY. — "We shall be pleased to offer special inducements in freight rates for the betterment of our public roads."

ATCHISON, TOPEKA & SANTA FE RY. — It has been the custom to make the rates on road materials very low, in order to encourage the building of good roads tributary to our line. Each case is handled on its merits as the question arises, and rates arranged in accordance with the circumstances of the case.

LOUISVILLE & NASHVILLE RY. — Have made reduced rates in so many cases to encourage road-building that it would be impracticable to recapitulate them.

WEST VA. CENTRAL & PITTSBURG RY. — Is anxious to do its utmost to encourage the construction of good public roads.

WABASH RY. — Have hauled material free, the local officials unloading the same.

WABASH, CHESTER & WESTERN RY. — Would make rates at bare cost of hauling or less.

WILMINGTON, NEWBERN & NORFOLK RY. — Would give half rates.

ILLINOIS CENTRAL RY. — Have reduced rates to encourage road-building and advanced the payment of our taxes for two years to assist localities.

HANNIBAL & ST. JOE RY.
ST. LOUIS & KEOKUK RY.
KANSAS CITY & COUNCIL BLUFFS RY.
CHICAGO, BURLINGTON & KANSAS CITY RY.
} It has always been the policy of these roads to make liberal concessions on material to improve roads.

ORANGE BELT RY. — Has furnished material free and reduced rates on transportation.

PITTSBURG, AKRON & WESTERN RY. — Would offer reduced rates or free transportation to encourage good road movement.

SAVANNAH, AMERICUS & MONTGOMERY RY. — Rates are very low.

ST. LOUIS, ALTON & TERRE HAUTE RY. — Would be glad to give reduced rates to encourage road improvements.

STUTTGART & ARKANSAS RY. — Would make very low rates if any movement was made toward road improvement.

TOLEDO & OHIO CENTRAL RY.
KANAWHA & MICHIGAN RY. } It is the policy of these roads to encourage road-building by very low rates of freight and furnishing facilities for handling road material.

CHICAGO & EASTERN ILLINOIS RY. — Will do all in their power to promote the construction of good roads. Will make very low rates.

ELMIRA, CORTLAND & NORTHERN RY. — Very low rates.

FALL BROOK RY. OF PENN. & N.Y. — Would offer reduced rates or free transportation if good material was offered for road-making.

INDIANA, ILLINOIS & IOWA RY. — Have offered to haul stone free to improve roads to depots, and always ready to co-operate in road improvement.

JACKSONVILLE, ST. AUGUSTINE & INDIAN RIVER RY. — Have always given one-half rates for road material. Will gladly assist in any way possible.

LAKE ERIE & WESTERN RY. — Take pleasure in making the rates as near actual cost as possible.

LOUISVILLE, NEW ALBANY & CHICAGO RY. — Would reduce rates one-half as an inducement to improve roads.

MIDDLETOWN & CINCINNATI RY. — Will assist all in their power.

NEW YORK, ONTARIO & WESTERN RY. — Have made half rates to induce road improvement and frequently subscribed money for improving roads.

NEW YORK, PHILADELPHIA & NORFOLK RY. — Always transport at reduced rates to improve roads leading to stations.

CHARLESTON, SUMTER & NORTHERN RY. — Have donated and delivered free the material for building a road at Sumter, S.C.

WILMINGTON, COLUMBIA & AUGUSTA RY. — Have donated and delivered free the material used for road improvements.

UNION PACIFIC RY. — "We are of course interested in the improvement of highways throughout the territory reached by our lines, but systematic effort in this direction is of recent growth. No reduced rates or free transportation has yet been asked for."

Central Penn. & Western Ry. — "We have never been called upon to make special rates for the transportation of road-making materials, but would do so to encourage road-building."

Penn. Lines West of Pittsburg. — This company is favorably disposed to encourage the building of good public roads, and will render what aid it consistently can.

These various companies, located in all parts of the country, have thus made, or offered to make, concessions in aid of road construction ranging all the way from "reduced rates" or "half rates" down to "bare cost of hauling or less," and even to "free transportation" and "free materials."

A fair average of these concessions would perhaps be the hauling at bare cost, and it would seem that if the companies could be brought to a united consideration of the matter, and with the prospect that their favorable action would result in a decisive movement for road improvement throughout the country, they might decide to make the "cost basis" universal. Precisely what this means or would amount to is of course uncertain; one president of a transcontinental road puts it at "one mill per ton per mile on straight and level roads," but it would be safer to double that rate, which would bring it nearly up to the present actual cost of moving coal. At this rate a yard of broken stone weighing 2800 pounds would be carried 100 miles for 28 cents, or for the cost of moving it one mile on our average roads by wagon. Such a rate of transport presupposes, of course, a very large movement and the best arrangements possible for quick loading and unloading.

Several of the railroad companies give the cost of crushed stone put on board their cars at 30 to 80 cents per cubic yard, and of gravel at 10 to 25 cents per cubic yard. Taking the former to average 50 cents, and the latter 15 cents, and the rates of hauling as above, it appears that road material can be delivered at any distance up to 200 miles at a total cost of $1.06 per cubic yard for stone, and 71 cents for gravel.

CHAPTER XIII.

ROAD MATERIALS IN THE UNITED STATES.

TAKING for granted the desire of the railroad companies to aid in the general improvement of highways, and their ultimate general consent to the establishment of such low rates for transport as will permit the movement of the small amounts of superior material needed for surfacing roads to distances reaching 200 miles, and of the inferior sort suitable for substructure, to a distance of 100 miles, it may safely be said that no considerable part of the United States will lack a ready and full supply of road material.

Glancing over the country somewhat in detail, and beginning in the far northeast, the State of Maine could surface all her roads with the chips from her granite quarries, and underlay them with the surplus stone from her fields; a large part of the remainder of New England needs only to run a portion of its stone fences through rock-crushers to have an endless supply of good material, and wherever the local supply fails, a very short railroad haul will permit making a selection from almost all the good kinds of rock.

In New York the entire canal region, not otherwise

provided for, can be supplied with its choice of trap, granite, limestone, or iron ore, from the Hudson River, carried at a minimum cost by the fleet of grain boats returning empty from the city, whenever there is demand enough to warrant making the necessary arrangements for the quick and economical loading and unloading of broken rock; the northern projection of the State has its own granite hills and boulders; the southern tier counties have abundant good gravel and rock, while at the point where "three States meet," New York, New Jersey, and Pennsylvania, is found a remarkable deposit of debris from the Hamilton sandstone cliffs, lying massed against the mountain on the west bank of the Delaware for a stretch of thirty miles, already "broken to sizes," and waiting only for the railroad and steam shovel, to furnish all the good road material that could ever be used in the three States, at the cost of loading and hauling.

New Jersey has the best of road metal in the trap rock of the Palisades and other dikes further west; Pennsylvania has rock in abundance, though much of it is unfit for use, and in many districts railroad transportation will be demanded. Maryland and Virginia have shells on the coast, and rock further inland. The Carolinas have clay enough to mend their sandy roads in the lowlands, and good stone in their upland regions. Georgia and Alabama have the same, and Florida has its coquina and clay. Mississippi has the Tishomingo gravel, an excellent material; Tennessee, the Chattanooga flints; and Kentucky, the famous Paducah gravel, which cements itself when laid. Ohio has limestone in abundance, and Indiana excellent gravel. Michigan has abundant good gravel in the southern half of the State, with some rock and boulders further north. Illinois has gravel and limestone in the north end of the State, and quarries of quartz in the south; while the great drainage canal, which is intended to turn a river out of Lake Michigan into the Mississippi, is already throwing up a mountain range of broken stones for a length of twenty-five miles, sufficient, with something better for surfacing material, to macadamize all the roads within a hundred miles. Wisconsin has granite, gravel, and coarser glacial drift. Minnesota has excellent quartzite in the southwest portion of the State, also granite and glacial drift in other parts. Iowa has some gravel and limestone, but neither is of the best quality except in the northern portion, and in limited areas elsewhere. Missouri has plenty of good road material, though it is not well distributed. The cherts or flints of Arkansas are excellent for roads, and will help to supply the near-by sections of Louisiana, Texas, Kansas, and Oklahoma. Southern Louisiana is provided with the Rosetta gravel; Texas has occasional beds of good rock, gravel, and shells; Eastern Kansas, some fair limestone; Nebraska has a very limited supply of good materials, but South Dakota, on the north, has plenty to spare and of the very best, the hard and durable jasper of the Sioux Valley. North Dakota has no good rock, but some drift deposits. The mountain States are well provided with rock, but, owing to their favorable conditions of soil and climate, have less need of it than the prairie States. The Pacific Slope is abundantly supplied, especially the States of Oregon and Washington. The Union Pacific R. R. Company reports of this region, "that along the Columbia River, from Portland to Wallula, along the Snake and Umatilla rivers, and most streams of any size, there are high basaltic bluffs, under which there are slopes containing vast quantities of broken basaltic rock of excellent quality for macadam. Much of this broken rock is small enough for use, and the remainder can be readily broken up into sizes required for road-making. In many cases these rock slopes extend down to our track, and the rock could be loaded on cars by steam shovel for ten or fifteen cents per cubic yard."

CHAPTER XIV.

THE BEST ROAD FOR A FARMING DISTRICT.

There is little difficulty in determining from experience what kind of road should be built between large towns, in village streets, or in city suburbs; and there is no great difficulty in getting the right kind of a road built in such localities; but in this country, so few good roads have been made in purely agricultural districts that experience avails but little in determining what will best serve the needs and suit the means of the farmer. In the first place, the road must not be too costly, or it will not get built; in the second place, it must be as good as the best for its purposes, when it is built, for the farmer should be able to do his heavy hauling over it when his fields are too wet to be worked and his teams are free.

The roads which have been built by counties have not always satisfied the farmers who had to use them. An enthusiastic Western worker for hard roads lost heart entirely and dropped out of the work, upon visiting a portion of Ohio and finding the country people travelling in the ditches to save the bare feet of their horses from the macadam roads. He did not stop to think that when wet weather came the same people would get their horses shod and thankfully travel over the hardest road they could find.

The road that seems to fill the farmer's eye, having in view all these considerations, is a solid, well-bedded stone road, but so narrow as to be only a single track, and having an earth track on one side. A visitor at the Road League headquarters in the World's Fair left this memorandum: "Forty years' experience on roads has given me this idea, that there should be a dirt road next to the gravelled road, as in the summer months the dirt road would be used in preference. Where a dirt road has been made alongside, the life of a gravelled road has been found to be five years longer. Dirt roads will keep the snow in winter while no snow will stay on the pike."

This recommendation was discussed by many subsequent visitors and very generally agreed to, and the specimen of very narrow stone road (eight feet wide) with the earth track alongside, exhibited by the League, was usually pronounced much the best for country roads; in fact, some farmers declared they would oppose the building of stone roads unless a dirt track was provided. It is quite true that a fine, dry, smooth dirt track is the perfection of roads: it is easy on the horses' feet and legs, easy on vehicles, and free from noise and jar. It is equally true that it holds snow better than stone or gravel, and requires less snow to make sleighing; and, where such a track has a stone road alongside to take the wear in wet weather, it will hardly suffer any appreciable wear. The stone road, on the other hand, wears by the grinding of the wheels and the chipping of the horses' calks in dry weather as well as wet; if it can be saved this wear for an average of six months in each year, so much will be clear gain.

The questions raised regarding this method of construction are, whether the junction of the earth and stone sections of the road can be kept even, so as not to have a jog in passing from one to the other, and how the meeting and passing of loaded teams is provided for. But practical experience has already been sufficient to settle both these points. The Canandaigua roads, some of which have been in use two or three years, show no sign of the division between the earth and the stone, and those who use them say that no difficulty is found in passing teams; it is only necessary for one of the wagons to run one wheel off the macadam; and since the earth portion of the road is never used when wet, it is always firm and smooth enough to permit doing this with ease.

On the whole, this appears to be a case in which "half a loaf" is not only "better than no bread," but better than a whole loaf. The purposes of a wide, hard road are better served by a narrow one, and all the objections to it removed, while the cost is cut down to a moiety, and the charges for repair lessened in even greater proportion.

CHAPTER XV.

THE BEST CONSTRUCTION FOR A NARROW, HARD ROAD. — SOME FARM ROADS IN ILLINOIS.

The cross-sections of the Canandaigua roads shown in Chapter III. give the simplest forms for narrow, hard roads; both these forms are symmetrical, having the stone road in the middle: one of them has a dirt track on each side; the other has none at all, only a shoulder of earth to keep the macadam in place. While the users of these roads are so pleased with the novelty of their hard roads that they do not seem to care for the dirt track, they will doubtless in future find their advantage in having at least one such track in all cases.

Where roads are already graded wide enough, it is better perhaps to have the three tracks, but two will serve all purposes of use quite as well. Two tracks will require a road-bed about 21 feet wide. In all wet soils or springy places there should be an underdrain beneath the stone track, as shown in Fig. 1, with side outlets at places where the necessary fall can be had. The space above the drain tile up to within six inches of the surface can be filled with any cheap, coarse material, first covering the tile with straw to prevent the earth washing into the joints. Field stone, common gravel, sand, or the burnt clay ballast used on some prairie railroads, will serve equally well for such filling. This should be well rolled and the road finished with a layer of the best broken stone or gravel obtainable, also well rolled, or, better still, with two layers of three inches each, rolled separately.

Where the underlying soil is naturally porous and the underdrain is not needed, the simple construction in Fig. 2 is all that is required, but the ground under the macadam should be well rolled and compacted, and all soft places excavated and filled with good material. If the ground is not porous, yet is not wet enough to warrant the expense of subdrainage, it is well to provide a drainage for the macadam bed in the form shown in Fig. 3; for, without entering into the controverted question whether the macadam is properly a "roof" or a "sieve," or disputing that the former is a "consummation devoutly to be wished," it is wise to be on the safe side and take away the water if it does get through; it certainly is wise to do this if it can be done at a slight cost.

All that is required for this is to give a slight outward slope to the bottom of the bed, roll the ground thoroughly, and provide an occasional drain through the earth shoulder into the ditch. These side drains should be provided in all low places in the road, and at intervals on all long slopes. They may be of tile, or better perhaps of wood, either tarred or charred to prevent decay.

The three-track road, Fig. 4, requires a road-bed about 27 feet wide; its construction corresponds to that of the two-track.

Another form of narrow, hard road is one used by Judge Caton of Chicago, on his Illinois farms.[1] While these roads are made for farm use, they would serve equally well for the lesser public roads of a neighborhood, and are worth a careful study with that view. The road is made by ploughing two furrows 16 inches wide and about 12 inches deep, under what are to be the wheel tracks, turning the earth inward, and two more for ditches, also turned inward, which results in a slight raising of the road-bed, then filling the inner furrows with field stones or coarse gravel and finishing with a light coating of fine gravel. Figures 1 and 2, respectively, show the road-bed prepared and finished. This plan gives a very solid bed of material under the wheels and a sufficiency elsewhere, and if occasional side outlets are provided, the furrows are quite efficient as blind drains. Occasional passing-places would need to be provided on public roads, for the meeting of loaded wagons; elsewhere, the width shown, 11 feet between ditches, would be sufficient for ordinary light travel. Such a road will use the minimum of material with the maximum of efficiency, and, having a great depth of stone just where it is needed, should bear the heaviest loads without injury, and require only an occasional resurfacing to last indefinitely. The amount of material required is less than 800 cubic yards per mile.

---

[1] Judge Caton has been for sixty years a prominent figure in the active public work of the Great West, not less distinguished in agriculture than in law, science, and business affairs; and he takes as great pride in his good roads as in the greatness of his crops.

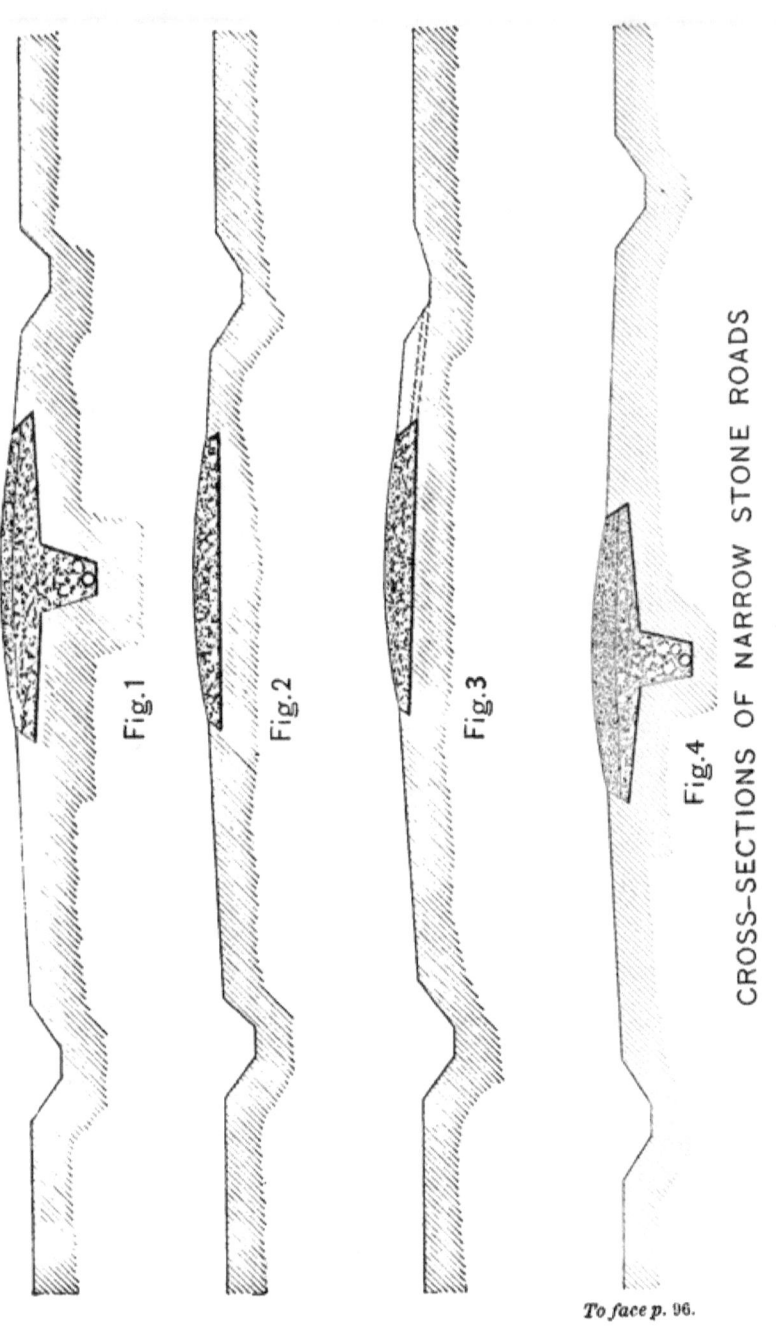

CROSS-SECTIONS OF NARROW STONE ROADS

CHAPTER XVI.

TREATMENT OF SANDY ROADS.

The usual way of mending sandy roads is to cover the surface with clay, or to mix clay with the surface sand.

The Massachusetts Highway Commission says it is "questionable whether this method of treatment is in the long run economical." The Commission estimates the average cost of doing this at 15 cents per square yard with renewal in about five years, or 3 cents a square yard annually, and says, "A good macadam road can be constructed for 60 cents a square yard; taking into consideration the small amount of travel, and that the road is estimated to last twenty years with hardly any repairs, the annual cost will be 3 cents per square yard, or the same in each case."

Other materials have been used for the more or less temporary hardening of sand roads, and some of them with marked success. For this purpose, any strong fibrous substance, and especially one which holds moisture, such as the refuse of sugarcane or sorghum, and even common straw, flax, or swamp grass, will be useful; spent tan is of some service, and wood fibre in any

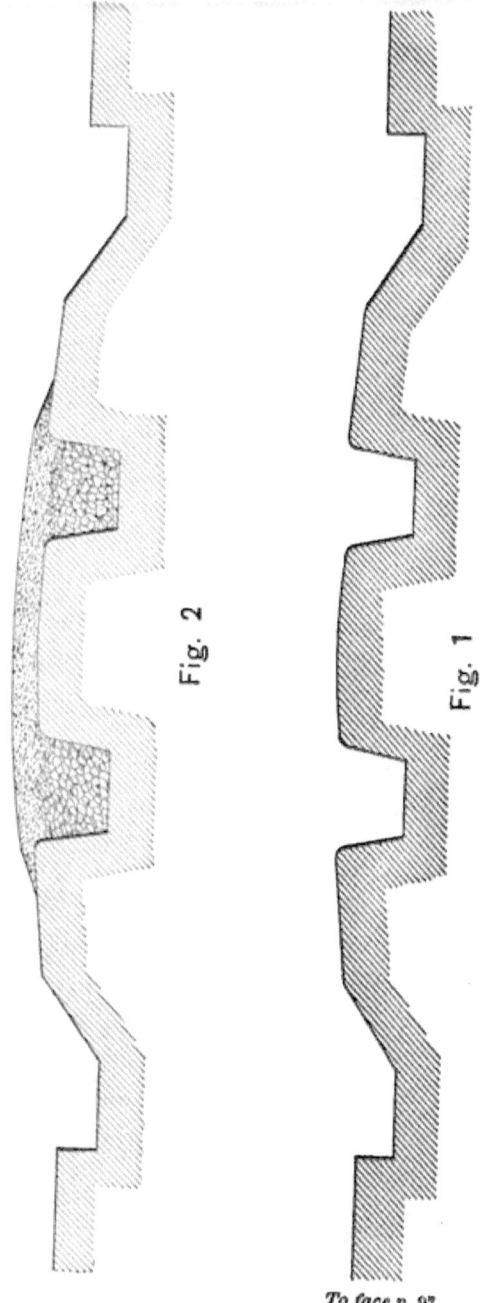

JUDGE CATON'S FARM ROADS IN ILLINOIS

Fig. 2

Fig. 1

To face p. 97.

form is excellent. The best is the fibrous sawdust made in sawing shingles by those machines which cut into the side of the block. This has been used to some extent in portions of Wisconsin, and its results are described in the following letter: —

"NECEDAH, JUNEAU COUNTY, WIS.
"December 1, 1893.

"MR. ROY STONE, WASHINGTON, D.C., —

"DEAR SIR: Yours of the 28th ult. is at hand, inquiring in relation to sawdust roads. The officers of this town, Necedah, have for several years past used shingle sawdust on the principal travelled roads in the town. The land is very sandy.

"Sawdust is first spread on the road from 8 to 10 inches deep; this is covered with sand to protect the road against fire lighted from pipes or cigars carelessly thrown or emptied on the road-bed. The sand also keeps the sawdust damp. The dust and sand will shortly become hard and packed; the wheels of the heaviest wagons make no impression upon it; it appears to be almost as solid as a plank road, but much easier for the teams.

"The road prepared in the above manner will remain good for four or five years and will then require renewing in some parts.

"How lumber sawdust would answer I don't know.

"Very respectfully,
"J. T. KINGSTON, P.M."

The ordinary lumber sawdust would of course not be

so good, but if mixed with planer shavings it might serve fairly well.

Another letter from an adjoining county confirms Mr. Kingston's statement, and details some experience with other methods, as follows: —

"FRIENDSHIP, ADAMS COUNTY, WIS.
"*December 21, 1893.*

"ROY STONE, ESQ., WASHINGTON, D.C., —

"DEAR SIR: Your inquiry as to the use of sawdust on sandy roads received; we have sandy roads in this county, but never use any sawdust on them; we use clay and marsh muck; clay we think makes the best road, when put on as it should be. After the introduction of wide-tire wagons (four-inch tires), we find little trouble with sandy roads. Very heavy loads are being hauled over the sandiest roads with no difficulty on four-inch-tired wagons, and I consider the use of wide tire on wagon and buggy of far more importance than any road filling that could be possibly done in this county with the means we have at our disposal for the work.

"In Juneau County some very fine roads have been made with sawdust; from Necedah to the Wisconsin River, a distance of about three miles, it is the boulevard of that county, and it is a pleasure to ride over that road in the nice summer day, but they have the sawdust handy by, and can fill the road cheap.

"In this county, where roads have been well graded and trenches about 18 inches wide and 10 inches deep filled with clay, and about 2 inches of sand on top just where the wheels run, it has made the best lasting roads for all kinds of use, and it is the very cheapest way we can make them.

"Various plans have been proposed, but none so good for the money as the above.

"Buckwheat, rye, and sorghum straw have been used with good results.

"Yours truly,
"C. M. SIMONS,
"*County Clerk.*"

CHAPTER XVII.

TREATMENT OF DIRT ROADS.

What has been said in the foregoing chapters clearly demonstrates that all the important roads of the country can be, and probably will be, macadamized or well gravelled in the not distant future, and this expectation should govern the present treatment of roads everywhere; no labor or expense should therefore be put upon them, more than is necessary to keep them usable, except such as, while it will secure their present betterment, will count also toward their ultimate improvement as hard roads.

For the latter purpose they will require attention, first, to their location; second, to grading; and, third, to drainage. If a road goes over a hill which it might go round, the labor put upon it is wasted, and the sooner it is changed, the better; if on the level it is not already well rounded up and surface drained, it should be, not only for present use but as a preliminary to macadamizing; and if it is not underdrained in all wet spots, that should be the first work done. Nothing, indeed, will pay better for present use than putting in good tile or stone drains, and they will count for all they cost in the future road-building; they should be put in wherever the subsoil is of a nature to hold water.

Hon. W. L. Webber, the Chairman of the Michigan Highway Commission, gives this instance of the benefit of drainage in Saginaw: "In this city, a few years ago, the Common Council placed the drainage of streets under the control of the Board of Public Works, by resolution; whereupon, the Board of Public Works at once let contracts for several miles of tile drains, upon which the Council promptly revoked the authority which had been given to the Board, the tile drains being regarded as an improvident use of the public money; but the contracts made were carried out, and after one year's experience the Council was so thoroughly satisfied of the advantage of the tile drainage in streets that, since that time, no street has been ordered improved without ordering tile drains in."

Mr. Webber further says: "Road-beds should be drained in all places where the subsoil is clay or packed, so that the surface of the road will have no standing water under it to a depth of at least three feet, and there is no one word which should be so thoroughly impressed into the minds of all connected with the making of roads, as the word '*drainage,*' *thorough drainage, deep drainage.*"

CHAPTER XVIII.

WIDE TIRES.

The Massachusetts Highway Commission, after a thorough study of this subject, reached this conclusion: "From our own observation, and from testimony in the different parts of the State, the wider tires offer many advantages which should commend their use to teamsters in general. There can be no question but that on the ordinary roads larger loads can be hauled with less strain upon the horses and less outlay for repairs on the equipments."

The Commission, however, recommended no State legislation on the subject, mainly on account of the cost of changing the 50,000 wagons in the State at $20 each, amounting to a million dollars, "a sum sufficient to construct about 200 miles of road of the kind which would not be likely to suffer from any width of tires used upon them," and they are of the opinion that as our roads are brought into a proper state the tire question will become unimportant. Apparently the legislature thought differently; for the Highway Manual of the State of New York, issued subsequently, says: "Massachusetts has recently passed a law making mandatory the use of four-inch tire upon wagons for heavy traffic." The same authority further says: "In Pennsylvania, team wagons are required by law to have tire at least four inches in width, and the rear axles are eight inches longer than the forward, so that the wheels can never track each other. In England, the roads are kept free from ruts by the use of wagons with axles of indiscriminate length, so that the wheels of one wagon will not track those of another, and the rear wheels are universally wider apart than the fore wheels. The New York Legislature of 1893 passed a law providing for a rebate of road tax equal to one-half the full amount, not exceeding four days, for the use of three-inch tires upon wagons drawn by two or more horses. This was a move in the right direction, but the width of tire should have been four instead of three inches. The great injury done by narrow-tired wagons to our roads, however expensively and durably constructed, would have warranted our legislature in compelling the use of wide tires upon all wagons designed to carry heavy loads. The wide-tired wheels, with the axles of unequal length so that the wheels will not track, under heavy loads, act as rollers and keep the road hard and well packed and always free from grooves and ruts."

The preponderance of testimony appears to be strongly in favor of wide tires and unequal axles, not only as economical of power in hauling, but as tending to improve the roadway and maintain its improvement.

The tendency, as roads are improved, to increase the loads moved over them up to the full hauling capacity of the teams used, puts the new roads to a severe test, and often before they are fully consolidated. On a new stone road in Camden County, N.J., the writer lately saw loads of 7500 pounds of manure, or an equal weight of farm produce, on wagons weighing themselves over a ton and having the ordinary narrow tires. These wagons were cutting ruts in the road of one to two inches' depth, and constant care was required to prevent worse injury.

This road had been built by contract, with a percentage reserved, and the contractors were still caring for it, filling the ruts and rolling it, and its condition showed the wisdom of this arrangement; for if it had been accepted and paid for when it was apparently finished, and left without special care through this open winter, it would have been sadly cut to pieces before spring; whereas, if the rutting could have been avoided by the use of wide tires and unequal axles, the travel would have benefited the road. It was claimed, however, by those who had watched the construction of this road, that the rutting was due to insufficient rolling of the lower courses of stone, and that this was proved by the fact that wherever the travel had been forced on to the road during construction and the material thoroughly compacted thereby, as it was laid, no rutting had occurred. The reason given for using narrow tires in that vicinity is that the wagons must track with the horse cars, in Camden and Philadelphia, or be at a serious disadvantage.

Very careful experiments with wagons of varying

width of tires have been made by the Studebaker Brothers, and the results are detailed in the *Good Roads Magazine* for March, 1893. These experiments prove that across fields a three-inch tire has an advantage over a one and a half inch, of one-eighth in starting a load, and one-seventh in pulling it after starting. This advantage, together with the lessened liability to cut through and kill the grass of newly seeded fields, must gradually lead to the introduction of wide tires for farm wagons, and when used on farms they will be used on roads. The tests also showed an advantage in starting a load on a hard road, of one-sixth in favor of the three-inch tire over the one and a half inch, and a small advantage in favor of a four-inch over a one and a half inch in starting and hauling over sandy and gravelly roads, but a slight disadvantage in the wide tires on muddy roads and block pavement.

The most thorough practical test, however, of the merits of wide tires with varying gauges, considered as road makers and menders as well as load-carriers, is in the experience of the Solvay Process Company, near Syracuse, N.Y., given in *Good Roads* for January, 1894. This company was persuaded by Mr. William A. Sweet, President of the New York State Road Improvement Association, to try the use of wide tires and unequal axles in hauling stone from the quarry to their works, a distance of four and a half miles, over what had been a very bad clay road. They improved the road by putting on "rough quarry refuse, and for a part of the distance field stones (from stone walls) were used, all hand broken to two-inch and three-inch sizes. These were covered with fine unsifted quarry chips, and a crown was given to the roadway with an elevation of about six inches in a width of 16 feet."

Three three-horse wagons were built, with four and six inch tires of varying gauges, and the rear wheels tracking outside of the front ones. The result is told by Mr. Power, one of the Board of Supervisors of Onondaga County: "The constant use of three of these wagons during the last three years has produced a smooth, compact, and regular surface between the quarry and our works, and the substantial crowning of the road has kept the surface well drained, and, therefore, dry and free from ruts. These wide tires and varying gauges excited a good deal of attention at the outset, and conflicting opinions were expressed regarding their utility. The result is eminently in their favor, and the general sentiment has grown constantly in favor of the use of these wagons for heavy loads. We haul loads continually, varying in weight from 8000 to 16,000 pounds, with no perceptible wear, weakness, or breakdown, either to the wagons or to the roads. The carts used at our works are varied in gauge, and all have given excellent satisfaction in keeping the roadway smooth. When these wagons were first put into use, the road was rough and rutty and the work of hauling was severe on the horses, but soon the broad tires began to roll and pack the road surface, and it is now difficult to exaggerate the great benefit these tires have produced in keeping the road smooth and hard, and the amount of labor they have saved in the work of hauling and repairs."

Mr. Power further says: "These wagons were all 'poled' for three horses, and the use of three horses tended to combine with the wide tires and varying gauges of front and rear axles to smooth down even the slightest ruts caused by wagons of narrow tires and ordinary gauge, of which there were and are very many in use on this road."

Confirmation of the foregoing views can be had from many quarters and on good authority. The Committee on Roads, of the Virginia Association of Engineers, says: "In relation to this subject, we would also suggest that legislative steps be taken in regard to the width of wagon tire. 'Broad tires are road-makers, while narrow tires are simply road-destroyers.' The State of Michigan set the example of a new era in road-making by enacting a law regulating the width of wagon tires. As an inducement, the law provides for refunding one-half of the annual road tax to every farmer who supplies his wagon with broad tires. We earnestly urge the Association to bring these matters before the next Legislature."

CHAPTER XIX.

THE REPORT OF THE OHIO ROAD COMMISSION.

If the late report of the Ohio Commission is, as some friends of good roads think it, a distinctly retrograde step in the march of road improvement, it is the only one taken by any State authority.

The Commission recommends to the Legislature to pass no new road laws, but to adopt a plan of masterly inactivity in the matter, mainly upon the ground that the extension of electric railways will greatly restrict the use of wagon roads and curtail the extent to which they need be built.

The *Engineering News* of New York takes the opposite view of this subject, saying: "We do believe, however, that, especially in the neighborhood of large towns and cities, the present rapid extension of suburban electric railways will in itself hasten the general improvement of all roads affected by them. These suburban lines, by connecting chains of villages and towns and increasing the facilities for travel, tend to enhance the value of country property as a place of residence, and as a consequence create a demand for better roads and make it easier to meet the cost of improvement."

This Commission, appointed by Governor McKinley under joint resolution of the Senate and House, was directed by the Legislature to "thoroughly investigate the whole subject of road construction and the cost of transportation over the various kinds of roads, including those operated by steam power and electric power as well as those operated by horse power; and to report to the Governor what the average cost per ton per mile now is by horse power, and what the approximate cost would be if artificial power should be substituted for horse power; and especially whether it is possible and advisable to construct country roads so that both cars and wagons can pass over the same road, propelled by either horse power or artificial power; also, the estimated cost of such combination roads as compared with the cost of roads established for horse power only, together with whatever recommendation they have to make as to the road laws of Ohio, or as to the enactment of any new laws by the Legislature of the State."

The Commission estimates the common roads of the State at 80,000 miles, and the cost of "suitable improvement" at $5000 per mile, an amount which the *Engineering News* says is "altogether too high," and which is in fact four or five times as high as the cost of some excellent hard roads in various parts of the United States. Moreover, 10,000 miles of these roads are already improved, and probably 30,000 more are not of such importance as to demand much improvement. So that $50,000,000 judiciously expended ought to give the State a good system of highways.

The Commission says that in some parts of the State the people do not "appreciate nor desire good roads." They say: "There are, undoubtedly, some places in the State where material for road-making is sufficiently abundant and cheap, but where the character of the population is such that they prefer the discomforts and loss occasioned by defective highways to the trouble and expense required to improve the roads. It is manifest that no legislation can or should alter such a state of affairs. It is not the province of legislation to change human nature, and where a community deliberately prefers to adopt a course of action that is opposed to its best interests, it should be left to its own devices."

This is a novel exposition of the relations of a State to its citizens. It is generally considered that to promote education is one of the primary duties of the State, and if any part of its people are so benighted as this, on a subject of such importance to their welfare, it would seem that duty, self-interest, and State pride would all conspire to urge the better-informed sections of the State to work a speedy reformation among them; and, since no lessons are so useful as object lessons, the most effective and persuasive teaching would be to help build some bits of good road in each of these districts. There cannot be a county in the State in which some neighborhood would not jump at the chance to have its market road improved on the New Jersey plan. That State, with an appropriation of only $20,000 for the first year, and only $75,000 subsequently, has done such a work of education in three years as will speedily result in lifting its rural population many degrees in the scale of comfort and prosperity.

The effect of such lessons is not less marked in some parts of the State of Ohio. Mr. Samuel Huston, County Surveyor, of Steubenville, said at the Road League office in Chicago: "We have a system of county roads, eighty-five miles in one county (Jefferson); they are built under State road law, making it optional for county or township. About twenty townships came in under this provision, and only two were left out; these two were glad to come in afterwards, at an extra cost for the delay, as they saw the advantage of good roads. We have a single-track road, and a dirt road on the side, but where hills are steep, we make full-width roads. County bonds are issued, at 6 per cent, to pay for the roads. Public sentiment is entirely in favor of good roads going on. Before we made our roads an object lesson, nearly every farmer was against the good-roads movement."

The Commission says: "There are counties in Ohio that have improved their roads at their own expense in the past; they have borne the burden willingly and are now enjoying the benefits. To tax these counties again for the purpose of building roads in localities where the people, through lack of enterprise or inability, have failed to secure good highways, is unjust and is discouraging to enterprise. Why should Logan County or Hardin County or Union County, in which turnpikes have been built by local assessment, be required to contribute money for the purpose of building roads in

Geauga County, where there is not a single mile of turnpike?"

To this it might be answered, that an enlightened self-interest would commend to the wealthy counties the policy of stimulating improvement in the poorer ones, to enable the latter to bear in time their proper share of the burdens of the State; and, again, there are many ties of blood, friendship, and business which cross county lines, and the people who confine their driving to their own county limits are few indeed. The Commission has done good service in collecting information regarding the cost of various kinds of transportation, and though it does not propose any further action or investigation, but confines itself to negative recommendations, it may be hoped that its report will stimulate private experiment in the direction of such "combination roads," and ultimately bring in a new era of rural rapid transit; meanwhile, it seems a pity to raise up obstacles to such immediate and substantial improvement of the ordinary highways as is progressing elsewhere in the United States, and thus to bring a great State to a standstill in the path of progress.

CHAPTER XX.

FARMERS AND THE ROADS.

It has been the fashion among some road-reformers to throw upon the patient and long-suffering farmer all the blame for the present evil condition of the highways; they enlarge upon his ignorance and his blindness to his own best interests, and fervently exhort him to open his eyes and mend his ways. He is supposed not to know a good road when he sees it, nor what he loses by a bad one, and to be firmly set against any change. This view is so far from being correct that it is not surprising if farmers as a class are irritated by it, nor that serious friction often occurs in public meetings on this subject. It may be true that a few old mossbacks cling to the ruts and stones that were "good enough roads for their fathers," and that farmers of more intelligence have at times protested against hasty legislation which might inflict undue burdens upon them; but no class of men are more awake to-day to the need of road improvement, or more anxious to find practical means for its accomplishment, than the thinking farmers of the country, whether within or without the farmers' organizations. In fact, the practical work done in this direction, so far,

To face p. 114.

On Church Road, one mile east of Merchantville. Telford Road, twelve feet wide and twelve inches thick, built by State Aid, 1893.

both in road construction and in legislation therefor, has been mainly wrought through their efforts and good judgment. The development of the New Jersey law, which has been so successful as to be considered a model for other States, has been the work of the active members of the State Agricultural Society, and the law has been administered by the President of that society, himself a practical farmer. The good roads in Canandaigua, N.Y., and many of those in Connecticut and other States were planned and built wholly by farmers, while the farmers' organizations have taken strong ground in favor of the general reform. The National Grange assembled at Concord, N.H., in 1892, passed unanimously resolutions supporting the National League for Good Roads, and the State Grange of New York has this year taken an advanced position in the matter, and charged its permanent Committee on Legislation to follow up the work. There is much yet, however, for the organized farmers to do in this direction.

Every Farmers' Club and every local Grange or Alliance might have its Committee on Roads, with a secretary active in gathering information, and especially in corresponding with those branches of their organizations which are located where road improvement is going on and the problem is being solved by actual experiment. With the knowledge thus acquired, the organizations would soon be in position to criticise or dictate legislation, to exercise wisely the full power due to their vast numbers, and to shape and direct the movement instead of awaiting with apprehension its results in other hands. When all the farmers in the country know what a few know now, of the benefits of good roads, and the ease of getting them, we shall be far on the way to having them everywhere. Another thing farmers can do to their great advantage is to accept and welcome the help that is ready to be given them by others concerned in the betterment of highways. Many Boards of Trade and commercial organizations have taken up the question with earnestness, but have been repelled and discouraged by the attitude of those most directly interested in its solution. The wheelmen have attacked the problem eagerly, in the hope of helping on the millennium of good roads, but have been charged with selfishly aiming to oppress the farmers that they may enjoy the results. Farmers must remember that to the merchants and the wheelmen is due the willingness of the towns and cities to aid largely in the building of country roads, and the fact that, in many parts of the country, city people lead this movement which the country people are slow even to follow. If the time comes when all the friends of good roads can work together in harmony, they can readily command the help of those who are now indifferent, and will then make short work of the undertaking; but the farmers, being the most powerful in numbers and most deeply concerned in interest, must take the leading part in organizing and harmonizing the forces enlisted in this great crusade.

The city man wants good roads, for the better supply of country products and the improvement of trade, and

Farm Teams on their way to market, Camden County, New Jersey, March 10, 1894. State Aid Road.

for the occasional pleasure of driving or riding over them, but they are not essential to his well-being. To the farmer and his family they are a vital concern of daily life, and fortune and happiness wait upon their coming. Farmers in America have an especial reason for taking up this crusade. In marketing their products they are forced every year into closer and more disastrous competition with the cheap labor of other countries,— and countries whose despotic governments can and do compel the building of good roads to cheapen the movement of products. In this country such compulsion is impossible, and national aid even is hardly thought acceptable. The farmers are left to their own devices and must work out their own salvation. They pay a mud tax, estimated on good authority at $280,000,000 a year, and a road tax, almost as useless, of forty or fifty millions more. Is it surprising that they are not happy and prosperous?

CHAPTER XXI.

THE WHEELMEN'S CAMPAIGN FOR ROADS.

In the battle for good roads, it would be folly, as well as injustice, not to recognize the great services of the army of wheelmen who have sprung to the front within a few years, and who have often maintained the fight alone, through many discouragements, though their interest in it seems trifling and casual in comparison with that of the mass of road-users.

When we consider, however, that, for his vehicle, the bicyclist is both driver and horse, and that on bad roads he suffers in person what we have always inflicted on poor dumb brutes, and is entitled, therefore, to speak and fight for them as well as for himself, it is not to be wondered at that he is found in the vanguard, nor is it surprising that his zeal sometimes outruns his discretion, and impatience prevents his keeping step with the slow march of his allies.

If the wheelmen are the light troops of the army, they nevertheless carry heavy guns when it comes to legislation, and their audacity stops at nothing. When the writer was urging the passage of a National Highway Commission Bill, in 1892, the Wheelmen's League, then in session at Washington, took up the affair, and were not content with personal work on the spot, but stirred up their home people, and instantly telegrams to members of Congress poured in from all parts of the country with such a rush as to startle both houses out of any indifference to the matter, and the bill passed one house immediately, and only missed it through want of time in the other.

The wheelmen have kept alive the agitation of this subject when, one after another, associations formed for the purpose among other classes of road-users, have fallen stillborn. Their literature has flooded the country, and their road committees have worked without ceasing. The *Good Roads Magazine*, which they support, has drawn upon the best talent of the country for its articles, and has reached a circulation approaching a hundred thousand copies.

Whenever the farmers shall be ready in any State to propose legislation for road improvement, the wheelmen will take care that the city members of the Legislature are not indifferent, and whenever the cities are called upon to aid in country road-building, they will move heaven and earth to have that call met. In short, they will render any service to the cause of good roads that a quick intelligence can discover and an earnest zeal can execute, and their aid will be welcomed by every citizen who takes that cause deeply to heart.

CHAPTER XXII.

THE ATTITUDE OF COMMERCIAL ORGANIZATIONS.

While only a few of the many commercial bodies in the country have taken definite action in favor of improving the highways, those few are among the most important, and there is no question of the hearty concurrence of all the others, whenever they see the occasion for their action.

The National Board of Trade and Transportation in 1892 resolved that "we recognize the exceeding poverty of the country, even amid its riches, in the universally deplorable condition of its public highways, and favor a system which will provide for their immediate improvement, under control of the State governments."

The Chamber of Commerce of New York adopted strong resolutions of the same character, and appointed the Hon. Chauncey M. Depew and General Horace Porter to represent the Chamber at the Chicago Convention for the organization of a National League for road improvement. Later, the Chamber heartily indorsed the purposes of the League, and Mr. Camp, of the Committee on Internal Trade and Improvement, expressed the general view of the members in saying that "the movement for good roads deeply concerns every commercial and financial interest in the land. We are handicapped in all the markets of the world by an enormous waste of labor in the primary transportation of our products and manufactures, while our home markets are restricted by difficulties in rural distribution which not unfrequently block all the channels of transportation, trade, and finance. This state of things has heretofore been thought irremediable, under our system of government; but good roads are not incompatible with self-government in France and Switzerland, and the National League for Good Roads believes that education and organization will make them possible here."

The League itself summarized the varied interests involved and the manner of their concern, in this language: "No person or association in the land can afford to neglect a movement so vital as this to the country's progress and prosperity; few, indeed, have not, in addition to their concern in the general welfare, some special interest, direct or indirect, in the condition of the highways.

"Apart from the acknowledged interest in good roads of the builders of wagons, carriages, bicycles, traction and farm engines and implements, of coaching and country clubs, coach and carriage owners, horse-breeders, etc., and of all merchants and manufacturers, in respect to the cheap and speedy distribution of goods and better collection of raw materials and money returns, there are many great semi-public institutions whose interests are deeply involved: railroads, in the equal distribution of their traffic through the seasons, securing constant employment of their force and equipment; telegraph and telephone companies, in the extension of country service; newspapers, in the expansion of their circulation through free delivery that will follow good roads; banks and bankers, in the quicker movement of capital in country business; fire insurance companies, in the ability to reach country fires with town apparatus; life insurance companies, in the prompt relief of the sick or injured, and in a general amelioration of physical and social conditions tending to prolong life; labor organizations, in the non-competitive employment of convicts; and all philanthropic associations, in the provision of employment sufficient to abolish want and starvation, for a generation, diminish crime and relieve the congestion in cities, and in the cheapening of food products to all consumers, and a general promotion of the happiness and welfare of the whole people."

Nothing need be added to this but for the active commercial friends of road improvement to urge upon the trade organizations of which they are members the expediency of taking prompt action in the matter, and of appointing permanent committees on the subject. The establishment of the Government Bureau will facilitate the work of all such committees in many ways, and make the collection of information easy. And when the 1300 commercial bodies in the United States are prepared to throw their united weight in favor of definite measures of road reform, the battle will already be half won.

To face p. 129.

CHAPTER XXIII.

ROAD-BUILDING AND THE REVIVAL OF BUSINESS.

THE present depression in business of all kinds, throughout the country, so far from stopping the agitation for good roads, or hindering the work of their construction, furnishes a new motive for the agitation and a rare opportunity for the work.

The National League, in September last, issued the following circular: —

"The earnest attention of members of the League, its co-workers, and all committees and persons seeking relief for the unemployed, is respectfully called to the present favorable conditions for *road improvement*, both for its own sake and as a means of giving employment and stimulating business in general.

"Capital, as well as labor, is idle, and bankers are expecting an era of cheap money, bringing a quick demand for such investments as town and county bonds.

"Many county and town boards in various States are already authorized to begin road-making and to issue bonds therefor; others require only the sanction of a local election.

"Men enough could be put to work by these bodies, without waiting for legislation, to give sensible relief to the labor market, and materially ease the hard times in their localities, while the roads would be built at a minimum of cost and of interest charges. Those States that have not adopted the modern ideas would hasten their legislation to avail themselves of the same advantages, and the whole country be lifted out of its temporary difficulties, by means certain to promote its permanent prosperity.

"To enforce these considerations upon the attention of the boards having power to act, and upon the people having right to vote such power, is the practical work of the hour. Those who are willing to join actively in this work in their localities are earnestly requested to communicate with the League at these headquarters, and to give full information regarding local conditions."

The "era of cheap money" has already arrived, and shows signs of staying indefinitely.

No prophet is bold enough to fix a date for the revival of business, though some light on the subject may be drawn from experience in like conditions. Speaking in 1876, during the great depression which followed the panic of 1873, in reply to the question, "When will business revive?" Senator Thurman of Ohio said: "All that is necessary is for a man to open his eyes and read the history of his country to know when it will revive. At intervals of about twenty years we have one of those things called a panic, followed by stagnation in business, the result of over-trading, over-production, of extravagance of all sorts and descriptions — extravagance in individuals, extravagance in corporations, extravagance in governments, large and small — until at last the bubble bursts, and then comes a season of retrenchment, of economy. And how long does that last? How long is it before debts are liquidated and a surplus is accumulated, so that there begins to be an upward tide in the business of the country? Never has it been less than four years in the United States.

"One of the first things that I can recollect when I was a very small boy, not higher than this desk, was the condition of monetary affairs in 1819. How long did that stagnation last? It lasted until 1823. Then business began to revive throughout the country, and a period of great prosperity followed. Then came the panic and suspension of 1837, and the great stagnation in business that followed. How long did that last before business revived and the country began to be prosperous again? Five years. Then came 1857, at an interval of twenty years, and business had not revived when the war broke out and changed the whole face of affairs. And now comes the stagnation of 1873, and nothing but time, economy, honesty, and retrenchment, will liquidate indebtedness and accumulate a surplus which will set business in motion again and make the country prosper once more."

A writer in one of the morning papers brings together reports of the business situation in this country in the years immediately following the panic of 1873, in order to show the course of business recovery after that financial disturbance. He sums up the result as follows: —

"It thus appears that the recovery from the collapse of 1873 did not fairly begin until the summer of 1877, or four years afterward, and was not complete until 1879, or six years afterward."

Should then the fifth great panic of the series, that of 1893, be like in its results to the other four, we may expect to spend the remaining years of the nineteenth century in "stagnation, retrenchment, and liquidation."

But history may not always repeat itself, and the genius of the age is bold enough to undertake any promising short cut to prosperity, regardless of all the landmarks of history and precedent. Unfortunately, the most of these short cuts yet proposed are by the way of inflation of the currency, which promises nothing but to drive out foreign capital and alarm home investors. Thurman himself, who was not always for sound money, ridiculed the idea that the effect of a panic could be overcome by inflating the currency.

It is not the lack of money, but the lack of circulation for it, that makes the hard times at present. The first effect of the panic was to take the money out of banks and hide it; the second effect was to take it out of business; the former was soon over, and the money has gone back to the banks for safe keeping, but the latter goes on. Confidence in the banks has returned, but confidence in business has not; the capital withdrawn from business, which gave employment to labor, is being added to the mass of bank deposits, and labor is turned adrift. Money is idle in banks, and workmen are idle at home. Employment for both is wanted, and neither can get it without the other; the deadlock is complete; money will not go back into the ordinary channels of employment, on account of the uncertainties of the future, and labor cannot employ itself.

To break this deadlock it is only needful to find a safe and profitable way to use money; and it need not be so very profitable either, for money is as eager as labor to be employed, and will accept small returns, if they are only sure.

Causes quite independent of the money panic have helped to bring about the present state of things. In particular, the gradual diminution of railway-building, in consequence of over-building, has, within a few years past, thrown out of employment, or forced into occupations already over-crowded, nearly all the men who were engaged in it. The number employed directly in railway construction, or collaterally in the manufacture of material, equipment, and supplies for new railroads, was, in 1887, according to the *New York Sun*, 800,000.

Of this vast army, all who are idle are a direct charge upon the public, which cannot let them starve; those who have found work have probably through their competition cut down the wages of others more in the aggregate than all they have themselves earned; this again, by lessening the purchasing power of still larger numbers, has diminished employment in other fields;

and thus in ever-widening circles, this one disturbance has spread disaster through all our industries.

Coincident with it, the fall in price of silver, and the substitution of machinery for hand labor in iron mining, have thrown thousands of miners out of work; the customary outlet for all spare labor, the opening of new farms on the public domain, has been closed by the almost complete occupation of the arable lands; the capital dislodged from railroad construction, mining, etc., which would in ordinary times have snatched the opportunity to avail itself of cheap labor in other enterprises, has remained locked up.

The effects of all this are seen in lower wages for common labor than have been known for a generation, and lower rates of interest for money on call than have ever prevailed for any length of time in this country.

Sixty and seventy-five cents per day for labor, and one per cent per annum for money, are rates we could not have dreamed of in America a few years ago.

But this situation, deplorable as it may be, is not without its especial opportunities. The conditions offer unusual inducements for the inception of permanent works of a public character, and through this means the general deadlock may measurably be broken.

Quite apart from the philanthropic motive of furnishing relief to the destitute, it is clear that the time to push public works with profit is when private enterprise drops out of competition with them.

If it be true that he who invents a new want is a benefactor of mankind, through the employment given in supplying that want, he certainly is one who finds the way to fill an existing want, and one so long felt and so universal that the country has despaired of its being filled, and who at the same time provides a new field of employment for men and money, and gives to a whole people the first lift out of the slough of despond.

The opportunity to do this offers itself to legislators in every State of the Union to-day. The natural sequence to railway-building is the building of feeders to railways. A system of good common roads is essential to the complete usefulness of the railways, and necessary in every way to the public welfare; the construction of such a system only waits on legislative action, and when fairly begun it will furnish as much if not more employment than did railway-building in its most active days.

Many believe it the duty of the State to promote employment, and the wisdom of giving work rather than alms to the able-bodied poor is undisputed; but in this matter we need not invoke any doubtful powers nor pretend to any benevolence, but look only to the narrowest and most sordid consideration, namely, that the State can drive a good bargain with its citizens in their time of need.

Some believe that the National Legislature should act in this behalf, but there are so many opinions on the subject, and so many questions, constitutional, political, and practical, involved in national action, that it would be folly to wait on their discussion and settlement, when the way is clear for the States to proceed at once. Not only is the way clear, but enough has been done by one State, at least, to point out a method of procedure that is easily practicable and already proven to be successful.

Many of the States have only got so far in their efforts at road-making as to find out "how not to do it"; but New Jersey, as we have seen, has found how to do it, and is rapidly putting that knowledge into effect, the secret of the method being in a neighborhood initiative and contributive, with voluntary State aid and compulsory county aid.

The justice and policy of State aid to road-building have been disputed, but the practical good accomplished by it in New Jersey is fast reconciling her people to it and inclining those of neighboring States to its adoption. New York and Pennsylvania are both moving in that direction. It is the only method through which the cities and corporations, which pay the bulk of our State taxes, can give the help which most of them are willing and anxious to give, towards the building of country roads. Should the other States adopt this method, they will find it easy to carry out. If they should need to borrow money for their portion of the expense, they are generally in excellent credit and can borrow at low rates. The counties can do the same; and if the local property-owners cannot pay their share at once, the counties can give them time to pay it out of the benefits realized, as cities do in the analogous case of street improvement.

The national government could do one thing to

stimulate and aid this work, and that without straining its powers or incurring any responsibilities. The need of new securities for bank circulation, in place of the rapidly maturing government bonds, is pressing upon Congress, and a variety of expedients have been suggested to meet this emergency. Among these are the acceptance, for this purpose, of county road bonds, limited in amount and guaranteed by the State. Such bonds would have the peculiar merit of multiplying their own security, since experience shows that every new road built adds many times its cost to the taxable values of the district in which it lies.

The State, having the taxing power, could always protect its own indorsement and save itself from loss.

With a proper limit to the issue of bonds, and a State supervision of the road-building, to insure an honest expenditure of the money, the State would run no risk, the government would get the best of securities, and the counties, by means of the State indorsement and the assured market for their bonds, would be able to borrow at so low a rate and on such time that the interest and sinking fund charges would be but a light burden. Probably the average rate of interest would not exceed three per cent per annum, and one-half of one per cent per annum in a sinking fund would pay off the principal in seventy-five years.

But to judge of the feasibility of this method of road improvement we must consider the combined weight of the State, county, and local taxation imposed by such improvement, as compared with the present taxation for road maintenance only. Taking the State of New York, for example: the total road mileage in that State is estimated by some at 100,000 miles, or 1 mile to each 300 acres of land; the present maintenance tax is $3,000,000 annually, or an average of $50,000 to each county, and of $30 for each mile of road, though of this amount probably five-sixths is applied to one-half of the roads, the other half being only neighborhood or by-roads. Properly to improve the important half, which is all that need be considered, would require an average expenditure of about $1500 per mile. This estimate may seem low, but it is two-thirds more than the cost of the stone roads of Canandaigua, N.Y. At this rate, the total for the State would amount to $75,000,000. Supposing the State and county each to pay two-fifths of the expense, and the respective neighborhoods one-fifth, the sixty counties would have to borrow $30,000,-000, or an average of a half million dollars each, for their own share, and a quarter million more temporarily, to carry the property-owners' portion until it could be paid.

The interest and sinking fund charge on the half million would be $17,500 per annum; but it is not too much to say that when the travelled roads of a county were well built, the saving in maintenance would be fully one-third of the present cost, which would practically meet this charge without increase of taxation, while the interest and principal of the quarter of a million would be paid by the local property-owners who borrow it.

The property-owners would pay one-fifth of $1500 per mile, or $300, which equals 50 cents per acre on the 600 acres of land which would on the average be benefited. This, if spread over ten years, would be 5 cents per acre, or, including interest, something less than 6 cents per acre annually.

If the State should borrow its $30,000,000 on the same terms, its annual share for interest and principal would be $1,050,000.

Since only seven per cent of the State taxes are paid by the farm property of the State, this charge would amount to less than a quarter of a cent per acre annually, and may be dismissed from consideration as bearing upon the farmer. The cities, corporations, inheritors, and others, who pay the remainder, will not feel it a serious burden in view of the vast compensations it will bring. The total is only about one-half of the proceeds of a comparatively new source of revenue in that State, the inheritance tax alone.

It appears, therefore, to be possible for the State of New York to abolish forever its "bad roads tax," which the State Highway Manual estimates at $1 per acre, or $30,000,000 annually, by the mere appropriation of one-half the inheritance tax, and by the voluntary action of the farmers in adding a little more than one-half to their present road taxes for the space of ten years.

What can be done in New York can be done elsewhere; and with the assurance that it is practicable, and will be profitable too, to build good roads generally and promptly throughout the country, it remains to be considered how this will effect an immediate revival of business.

For those who have watched the wave of agricultural prosperity which attends the mere grading of a railroad, through a difficult country, no explanation on this point is needed. For that work every farmer turns out a "scratch team" and receives more ready money from the earnings of "the boy and the colts" than he has done from his farm products for many years, while everything he raises finds a home market for a year or two at good prices.

The expenditure of $50,000 of outside cash in an average township, for road improvement, not only means good times while it is going on, but will make important additions to the permanent business capital of the township.

It means, moreover, the payment of debts, the revival of local trade, and, when it becomes general, the increase of the purchasing power of the entire agricultural class,—a class which, being largely freed from expense for food, can devote a much greater share of its cash income to the purchase of manufactures than can those whose food supply is a daily fixed charge upon their earnings.

Increased purchases by the farmers mean increased employment for the artisan class, thereby adding to their power to purchase farm products, and when it is once begun, this action and reaction brings prosperity to producer and consumer, including full employment to all who are engaged in the exchange and transportation of products. It is only necessary to set the ball rolling, and the place of all places to start it is with the farmers; money expended among them will quickly find its way through all the channels of trade and production. It would be worth while, at this crisis, even to make some sacrifices for this purpose. How much more is it worth while to bring it about by inaugurating a work of the highest beneficence, or, as the National League puts it, "to lift the country out of its present difficulties by means which are certain to promote its permanent prosperity."

The extent of roads in the United States is estimated at about one and one-half millions of miles. The cost of improvement will average higher elsewhere than in New York, which has good materials well distributed; it may be taken generally at about $1800 per mile. To improve one-half of the roads in the country at that rate would cost $1,350,000,000. This is a vast amount, but it would be less difficult to raise it for roads than for railroads, and it would be easier to expend it within a given time, the area of operation being wider and construction so much more simple. If this sum were expended for that purpose before 1900, it would not quite equal the expenditure for railroads in the same length of time prior to 1890, but it would be better distributed and ought to go far toward restoring general prosperity; certainly, with that amount of money put into circulation, and good roads everywhere, we might make shift to travel comfortably if not gaily into the new century.

In view of all the conditions, the friends of road improvement should now be able to enlist the great financial and commercial interests of the country in their cause. They will find opposition in some localities to the incurring of debt for road-making, but they can cite the experience of many counties and townships in New York, New Jersey, Ohio, Pennsylvania, Michigan, Indiana, and Kentucky, where such "borrowing" has brought, not "sorrowing," but relief and rejoicing, and they can say with truth that no instance to the contrary has come to the knowledge of the National League or been developed by the government inquiry. If any man doubts the practical value of road improvement, let them persuade him to visit the counties of Camden and Burlington in New Jersey, and he will find farming communities actually getting rich in these hard times, solely by reason of their good roads.

APPENDIX.

ABSTRACTS OF NEW ROAD LAWS IN SIXTEEN STATES.

CALIFORNIA.

Law of 1893.

1. Board of supervisors divide the county into road districts, and each supervisor is road commissioner in his district. *Road districts.*

2. Board of supervisors have control of all roads, and as road commissioners, they take charge of all repairs. They receive 20 cents per mile, one way, for travelling on this duty, but not to exceed $300 per annum. *Board of supervisors; duties; compensation.*

INDIANA.

Free Gravel Road, Law of 1893.

1. County commissioners, upon petition of fifty freeholders of any township or contiguous townships containing an incorporated town or city of less than 30,000 inhabitants, for the improving of any road by grading, paving, mecadamizing, or gravelling, shall submit the question to the voters of the township, towns, and cities on the line of the road, and if the majority of those voting are in favor of such improving, the commissioners shall proceed to build such road at once. *Question of road improvement to be submitted to voters.*

2. The petitioners to pay all costs of election. *Costs.*

3. Construction to be let to the lowest responsible bidder. *Construction.*

Bonds.	4. County bonds running from one to five years to be issued for construction of the roads.
Special tax.	5. These bonds and interest to be paid by special tax upon the property of the townships, towns, and cities on the line in proportion to the cost of the road in each.
Free gravel roads	6. Free gravel or stone roads may be built on county lines and their cost assessed upon the lands within 2 miles on each side.

MASSACHUSETTS.

HIGHWAY COMMISSION AND STATE ROAD LAW OF 1893.

Highway commissioners; duties, salaries.	1. Governor and council appoint three commissioners, at a salary of $2000 each and travelling expenses. Commission to compile statistics, make investigations, advise regarding construction, alteration, and maintenance of roads, prepare maps showing location of road materials, and hold a public meeting in each county for the discussion of road matters at least once a year.
State highways.	2. Upon petition of county commissioner the commission may adopt any road as a State highway, and construct the same if the legislature makes appropriation therefor, except that the grading and bridging shall be done by the county. Such highway to be maintained by the State under supervision of the commission.
Connecting roads.	3. Upon petition of two or more cities or towns a connecting road, new or existing, may be made a State highway, and constructed in the same manner.

MICHIGAN.

COUNTY OPTION LAW, 1893.

Electors vote on adopting road system.	1. The board of supervisors of any county may, by a two-thirds vote of all the members of said board, submit the question of adopting the county road system to a vote of the electors of such county.

2. In any county where the county road system shall be adopted, a board of county road commissioners, not exceeding five in number, shall be elected by the people of such county. *County road commissioners.*

3. Said board of county road commissioners may lay out such new roads within the county as they deem necessary. *Duties.*

4. Any road heretofore laid out, or any part thereof, shall become a county road if the board of county road commissioners shall at any time so determine. *County roads.*

5. Said board of county road commissioners shall determine the amount of tax to be raised. Such tax shall not exceed $2 on each $1000 of the assessed valuation. *Tax, raising.*

6. Whenever the board of supervisors of the county shall, by a two-thirds vote of all the members, resolve to contract indebtedness or issue bonds to raise money for the construction and maintenance of county roads, the question shall be submitted to a vote of the electors of the county at a general or a special election to be called for that purpose. . . . No bond or evidence of indebtedness shall be negotiated at less than par and the accrued interest. *Bonds, issue of; question to be submitted to vote of electors.*

NOTE. — The constitution of Michigan was amended in 1892 to permit this legislation.

MISSOURI.

LOCAL OPTION LAW OF 1893.

1. A majority of the legal voters voting may adopt the county system; whereupon, *County system.*

2. County courts appoint supervisors of roads. *Supervisors.*

3. County courts provide for working, repairing, and improving all public roads in the counties by contract. *Improving roads.*

4. Supervisors shall inspect the work and repairs contracted for and make quarterly reports to the county court, showing the condition of roads in the several districts. *Quarterly reports.*

5. County courts may establish tollgates upon any roads that may be gravelled, macadamized, or planked in a substantial manner. *(Tollgates)*

6. Whenever any citizen subscribes fifty (50) dollars or more for the purpose of improving any road, the county court may subscribe a like amount. *(County court may subscribe.)*

7. Poll-tax of $2 and property tax of 10 to 20 cents per $100, payable in money for county road fund. *(Poll-tax.)*

NEW HAMPSHIRE.

Road Law, 1893.

1. Each town shall constitute one highway district; all subdivisions are abolished. *(Highway districts.)*

2. Each town shall raise twenty-five (25) cents per $100, and as much more as may be deemed necessary for road purposes, but not more than fifty (50) dollars per mile of road. *(Funds, raising.)*

3. Each town elects highway agents, who have charge of the construction and repairs of highway and purchases. *(Highway agents.)*

NEW JERSEY.

Road Laws, 1888 to 1892.

1. The roads of a township are placed under the management of the township committee, and money may be raised by township bonds for grading, macadamizing, and improving the same; bonds to be authorized by vote of the annual town meeting. *(Township committee.)*

2. The board of chosen freeholders of any county may designate certain roads as county roads and improve the same by the issue of county bonds. *(County bonds.)*

3. The State shall pay one-third of all cost of road improvement so authorized by the chosen freeholders, within the limit, at present, of $75,000 per annum. *(State aid.)*

4. Whenever the owners of two-thirds of the lands fronting on any public road will undertake to pay *(Chosen freeholders may improve roads.)*

one-tenth of the cost of improving such road, it shall be the duty of the board of chosen freeholders to cause such improvements to be made.

5. The office of overseer of highways is abolished. *Abolished*

6. All road taxes are to be paid in money. *Road taxes.*

NEW YORK.

County Road Law, 1893.

1. The board of supervisors may adopt the county road system and designate county roads. *County road system.*

2. A county engineer to be appointed in every such county by the board of supervisors. *County engineer.*

3. County roads to be maintained at the county charge. *County charge.*

4. County engineer to have full supervision of construction and maintenance of county roads. *Construction of roads.*

5. Board may borrow money for construction, maintenance, and repair. *May borrow money.*

6. May issue bonds for twenty years bearing 5 per cent interest, but not to be sold below par. *Bonds.*

7. All road taxes in such counties to be paid in money. *Road taxes paid in money.*

Additional laws provide for an experiment in the use of convict labor on highways near Clinton prison, and for the publication of a manual containing the highway laws of the State and giving instruction in road-making. Copies to be furnished to each commissioner and overseer of highways at the town charge.

NORTH DAKOTA.

County Road Fund Law, 1893.

In addition to all other taxes for highway purposes a special tax on all property in the county, except in incorporated towns and cities, may be collected and kept as a county fund for the improvement of the principal thoroughfares in the county under direction of the county commissioners. *Special tax for road improvement.*

OREGON.

County Road Law, 1893.

County court may improve roads.
1. The county court of any county is empowered, upon petition of a majority of the resident landholders within 3 miles of the proposed improvement, to improve, change, grade, drain, gravel, or macadamize any county road or public highway.

Road viewers.
2. Viewers are appointed by the court to apportion the estimated cost upon all the side lands within 3 miles, according to the benefits derived therefrom.

County fund to pay one-half.
3. If the county court be satisfied that the proposed improvement will justify an expenditure from the county fund, it may order that a portion of said cost, not exceeding 50 per cent. shall be so paid.

Free.
4. All roads built under provisions of this act are free of toll.

Special tax.
5. The county court may levy a special tax of 50 cents per $100, and a poll tax of $2 per head, as a fund for building and maintaining county roads and bridges.

Day's work.
6. Petitioners for county road must each do one day's work on the road or pay $2 to the supervisor.

TENNESSEE.

Road Laws of 1891.

Road districts.
1. County courts divide their counties into road districts and choose commissioners for each district.

Duties of commissioners.
2. Such commissioners control highways and purchases in their district, and direct the manner of working roads.

Overseers and tools.
3. Commissioners appoint overseers and purchase necessary tools and materials.

Convicts may be employed.
4. All persons confined in county jails or workhouses are available to the commissioners for the purpose of working on the public highways.

5. The county court may assess the number of days' poll-tax from four to eight, and a highway tax from 5 to 25 cents on $100. — *Tax.*

VERMONT.

Road Law of 1892.

1. Creates the office of road commissioner for each town. — *Road commissioner.*

2. Lays a town tax of 20 cents on the dollar of the grand list,[1] and a State tax of 5 cents on the dollar for support of the highways; the State tax to be apportioned and repaid to the towns according to road mileage. — *State and town taxes.*

The law of 1893 creates a State highway commission to investigate the matter of road-building in the State. — *Highway commission.*

WASHINGTON.

Road Laws, 1890 to 1893.

1. Commissioners of any county may cause to be established or improved any public road or highway; — *Commissioners may improve roads.*

2. They may submit to the voters of such county the question of issuing bonds; — *Election.*

3. Such bonds to run not more than twenty years, and not to exceed 6 per centum interest; and — *Bonds.*

4. Not to make the accrued indebtedness exceed 1½ per cent of the value of the taxable property in the county. — *Indebtedness.*

5. Bonds to be sold at not less than par. — *Par value.*

6. A State road through the Cascade Mountains to be built under authority of a special commission. — *State road.*

WISCONSIN.

Road Laws of 1893.

1. The town board of each town shall have full supervision, management, and control of roads in said — *Town board, duties.*

---

[1] The "grand list" is 1 per cent of the valuation of property.

K

town, and may make and repair the same by contract, and appoint a competent superintendent of roads.

Purchase of material, etc.; pay.

2. The town board may procure machinery and material, and hire laborers and teams; may purchase gravel pits, stone quarries; may make temporary loans on the credit of the town, to be paid from the road taxes.

Pay taxes in money.

3. All road taxes to be paid in money, except in townships which specifically vote to retain the labor system.

KENTUCKY.

The Fiscal Court of each county to have full charge of roads. To levy a tax not exceeding 25 cents per $100 on property, and a poll-tax not more than one dollar, and a labor tax not more than six days. To appoint a county and district supervisors.

NORTH CAROLINA.

County commissioners and justices of the peace may provide a county fund for roads by a tax not exceeding 15 cents per $100, and four days' poll-tax. All jail prisoners and State prisoners for a term of less than five years, and all vagrants, are available for highway work, and courts may sentence convicts to hard labor on the public roads not exceeding ten years.

County commissioners have full control of expenditure for the county road fund.

PROPOSED LAW FOR STATE AID IN NEW YORK.[1]

Nos. 1164, 1405.

IN ASSEMBLY,

MARCH 9, 1894.

Introduced by Mr. KERR — read once and referred to the committee on agriculture — reported from said committee with amendments — ordered reprinted as amended and placed on the order of second reading.

AN ACT

To Provide for the Construction of Roads by Local Assessment, County and State Aid.

The People of the State of New York, represented in Senate and Assembly, do enact as follows:

SECTION 1. Petition of bordering land-owners for survey and estimate of cost of local road; subsequent petition of residents of benefit district. On presentation to the board of supervisors of any county of a petition signed by the owners of not less than one-third of the lands bordering on any section of road already established or proposed to be established in such county, asking for a survey and estimate of the cost of building or rebuilding such road in a substantial and permanent manner either of stone or gravel as prescribed in such petition, such board of supervisors shall cause such survey and estimate to be made for the information of such petitioners, and shall forward a copy thereof to the State engineer. Whenever, thereafter, the petitioners shall present to such board of supervisors a map or description of the lands which, in their opinion, will be directly benefited by the construction or improvement of such road, together with a written request of the owners of three-fifths of such lands, that all the lands so benefited and the personal property in such district be assessed, in proportion to the benefits conferred for such construction or improvement, to the amount of one-third of the total cost thereof, such board of supervisors shall cause such road to be constructed or improved.

[1] This bill passed in the Assembly by a vote of 84 to 23.

Such lands so mapped or described shall be known as the benefit district of the said section of road. But whenever the original petition in any case shall set forth that the area to be benefited by the road is peculiarly restricted by the proximity of other roads or by other circumstances, an examination and report shall be made by the supervisor of the town and the surveyor of the road, and if it appears thereby that such area is less than two square miles for each mile of the road to be built, then the proportion of cost required to be paid by the benefit district shall be diminished at the rate of three and one-third per cent of the whole cost for the first one hundred acres of such deficiency, and three per cent for each additional one hundred acres of said deficiency, but shall in no case be less than one-tenth of the whole, and the balance of the cost of such construction shall be equally borne by the county and State.

SEC. 2. Applications. — Copies of all maps and descriptions and requests of property owners residing within the benefit district accompanied by an application for State aid shall be transmitted to the State engineer, who shall file the same in his office and record the date of the receipt thereof. State aid shall be accorded to the various benefit districts in the order of the date of the receipt of their applications, and when such applications shall be sufficient to exhaust the appropriation made for such purposes, the State engineer shall notify the applicants and the county board of supervisors and all liability for State aid shall thereupon cease. Whenever any subsequent appropriation is made it shall be first available for the applications already on file in the order of their receipt. No State aid shall be allowed to any section of road unless the State engineer shall certify that such road is or will be a main travelled road and a proper subject to receive State aid.

SEC. 3. Construction of road. — Such road shall be constructed or improved according to plans and specifications furnished by the State engineer and shall conform to the survey and estimate of cost provided by the board of supervisors. The contract for such construction or improvement shall be let by the board of supervisors to the lowest bidder upon the publication of a notice once in each of four successive weeks in two newspapers published in such county stating where a copy of the plans and specifications of the proposed construction or improvement may be obtained, and the time and place where the board of supervisors or a committee thereof will meet to receive bids. The cost of the publication of such notice shall be a county charge. Each of such bids shall be accompanied by a bond, with satisfactory security in a sum to be determined by the board of supervisors, conditioned that if the contract shall be awarded to such bidder he will execute an agreement, in writing, to perform the work according to the plans and specifications and terms of the contract. Such contract shall be executed in duplicate by the chairman of the board of supervisors under the direction of the board, one of which shall be retained by the contractor and the other filed with the clerk of the board. A copy of each contract shall be forwarded to the State engineer to be filed in his office. Before beginning the construction of the work under any contract the State engineer shall appoint a competent person as superintendent of such work, who shall receive as compensation a sum not to exceed four dollars per day, to be paid in the same manner as other employés in the State engineer's department, out of the moneys appropriated for that purpose. Such superintendent shall supervise all work done under the contract and require the provisions thereof to be strictly adhered to by the contractor. The contract may provide that partial payment shall be made to the contractor during the progress of the work, in which case such superintendent shall, as each payment becomes due, make a certificate to the chairman of the board of supervisors, stating the amount of work done and that such work has been done according to the provisions of the contract, and thereupon such chairman shall direct payment to be made by the county treasurer to an amount not exceeding eighty per cent of the value of the work performed. When the work under the contract shall be fully completed the superintendent shall make a detailed and itemized statement, in duplicate, of the cost of the construction or improvement, one copy of which shall be filed with the secretary of the board of supervisors and one with the State engineer. When such roads are completed they shall become county roads and thereafter be maintained at county expense.

SEC. 4. County engineer. — A county engineer may be employed by the board of supervisors whenever required under the provisions of this act. Such engineer shall have general supervision of the construction of all roads built under this act, and shall have power to suspend any superintendent of construction appointed by the State engineer, for neglect of duty or incapacity, subject to the final action of the State engineer; during such suspension he may appoint a substitute, who shall be entitled to the pay of such superintendent.

Sec. 5. *Payment of cost of construction.* — Except in cases where the benefits are "peculiarly restricted," one-third of the total cost of the construction or improvement of such road shall be paid by the owners of the land and property in the benefit districts, which amount shall be assessed upon such owners according to the benefits derived by them; one-third shall be a county charge, and the remaining one-third of the total cost shall be paid from the State treasurer to the county treasurer, upon the warrant of the comptroller and the certificate of the State engineer that the road has been properly constructed according to plans and specifications furnished by him.

Sec. 6. *Assessment of cost upon property benefited.* — The assessors of each town, through which the road so constructed or improved extends, shall one year after the completion of such road assess the amount to be paid by the property owners of the benefit district upon the parcels of land and personal property therein, in proportion to the benefits conferred by such construction or improvement. They shall describe in the annual assessment-roll, in a place separate from other assessments, the several parcels of land so assessed, and set down the name of the owner of such parcel, when known, with the amount in dollars and cents assessed on each parcel. Such assessment shall be a part of the annual assessment-roll, and shall be subject to review and correction in the same manner as the annual assessment-roll, and the sums assessed on the several parcels of land shall be liens thereon respectively until paid, and shall be collected in the same manner as other town taxes, except that each assessment may be paid in ten equal annual instalments, with interest annually at the rate of five per cent on the amount unpaid, or in one instalment, at the option of the owner of the property assessed; but the owner may, at any time, pay the entire amount unpaid with interest to the date of payment. The amount remaining unpaid upon each assessment shall each year be added in like manner to the assessment-roll. All moneys collected upon such assessment shall be paid to the county treasurer and held by him as a separate fund for the payment of all claims arising from the construction or improvement of such road.

Sec. 7. Issue of bonds.— The board of supervisors of any county may borrow money, from time to time, for the construction and maintenance of roads built under this act, and may issue bonds or other evidences of indebtedness of the county therefor, which shall be under the official seal of the county treasurer, and signed by the chairman of the board of supervisors. Such bonds or other evidences of indebtedness shall bear a rate of interest not exceeding five per cent per annum, shall not be for a longer period than fifty years, nor be sold for less than par. But the amount of such bonds or evidences of indebtedness issued by any county for the purposes of this act shall not exceed three per cent of the assessed valuation of the real and personal estate subject to taxation in such county.

Sec. 7. This act shall take effect immediately.

PROPOSED STATE AID IN PENNSYLVANIA.

ONE MILLION DOLLARS ANNUALLY.

[Extract from the report of a commission composed of three senators, five members of the house, and five citizens, appointed by the governor — 1891.]

Your commission desire to say that in formulating a bill they have not attempted to give you one that will place the management, construction, and repairs of the roads, highways, and bridges of the Commonwealth on the highest and most scientific plan, but that they have endeavored to give you one that they believe will be, if enacted into a law, a long stride in advance of the present system.

They believe, at the same time, that it will not be so far in advance that the people will not adopt it.

Your commission has constantly kept in view the fact that in all reforms it is absolutely necessary to move in a conservative way, and thus create sentiments that will in the end produce the best results.

In the bill your commission herewith present to you, they have preserved the township as a unit, believing that the people will never surrender the township government, as it is the basis of our State organization.

The bill provides for three supervisors to be elected in each township for the term of three years, one of whom shall be elected each year, and they, like our school directors, to serve without compensation.

These supervisors are to have charge of the making and repairing of the roads, highways, and bridges, the appointing of roadmasters, and the fixing of their compensation, and also the compensation of the laborers under them.

Your commission believed that this method would, in a large degree, take the management of our roads out of politics, and thereby secure the very best men as supervisors, and enable the roadmaster to carry on his work in a business-like way.

The bill provides for a money tax, which it was believed would alone result in a reduction of at least one-half in the road tax of every township and at the same time give better roads.

In adopting a money tax no citizen of the township who honestly desires to work out his road tax is excluded from so doing, for provision has been made whereby preference is to be given to citizens of the township, between the ages of eighteen and fifty-five, and that no person who is not a naturalized citizen can be employed upon the roads of any township in the Commonwealth.

The bill further provides that the board of supervisors of a township may, if it is so desired, sell the repairing of the roads of the township to the lowest bidder or bidders, requiring the purchaser to give bonds in double the amount of the purchase, to carry out his contract under the specifications laid down by the board of supervisors.

Your commission were led to insert this provision in the bill to enable those townships that have such a system to continue the same, and to authorize other townships to adopt it if they so desire.

A large number of the members of your commission believed that by the selling of the roads for repairs there would be a great improvement in our roads, and, at the same time, a large saving in the cost thereof. Your commission at the same time believed that it was wise to allow each township to choose either plan, as in the judgment of the citizens thereof seemed best. Your commission fully realized the depressed condition of agriculture at the present time, and the over-heavy burdens the farmers of the Commonwealth are now bearing, owing to the unequal taxation under our present revenue laws. Your commission were therefore a unit in believing that if there were to be substantial and permanent improvements in our highways, there must be State aid, which they recommend. By permanent improvement is meant the use of stone, brick, slag, iron, gravel, wood, or other lasting material conveniently to be had.

Whilst an appropriation clause could not be inserted in the road bill, your commission have prepared another bill providing for one million dollars annually, to be distributed to the townships on the basis of the amount of road tax collected in each township the preceding year, and only on condition that the township shall lay aside twenty-five per cent of its road tax annually for permanent improvements, and that the twenty-five per cent shall, together with the State appropriation, be used only in stone or other permanent improvements of certain roads, which shall be designated highways.

Your commission have also provided for the election by each county of a suitable person, to be styled a county engineer, who shall have supervision of all roads on which State money is expended, and, in addition to that authority, shall be one of the jurymen in laying out of new roads, and the changing and vacating of old ones, but not to have any control over the other township roads; neither has he the power to expend the money on such roads.

The board of supervisors has the power to make the contracts for building these highways, and can alone expend the moneys received from the State, and the twenty-five per cent of the township tax added thereto, all of which must be paid into the township treasury, and over which the county engineer has no control whatever.

In providing for a county engineer, we believed it to be absolutely necessary that the State should be protected in its part of the work, and know how its money was being expended, as sacredly as the township.

Whilst the provision for a county engineer will entail the cost of another salaried officer, they were led to believe that it would be a great saving to the township, and thus save the counties many thousands of dollars, and at the same time give much more uniformity to our roads, and the making of the same.

Your commission believed that the engineer could from time to time hold supervisors' institutes from place to place in his county, and instruct supervisors and roadmasters in reference to the best methods of making roads, and also inform them of the progress being made in other parts of the county, and thus the people would become interested and stimulated to make more improvements.

To protect the interests of the people, we have introduced a section making it a penal offence for any supervisor or county engineer to be interested, directly or indirectly, in the making or repairing of roads, highways or bridges, or in the sale of materials used.

STATE HIGHWAY COMMISSION.

LAW OF MASSACHUSETTS, 1893.

[CHAPTER 476.]

AN ACT to provide for the appointment of a highway commission to improve the public roads and to define its powers and duties.

Be it enacted, etc., as follows:

Highway commission, duties, compensation, office, etc.

SECTION 1. The governor, with the advice and consent of the council, shall, within thirty days after the passage of this act, appoint three competent persons to serve as the Massachusetts Highway Commission. Their terms of office shall be so arranged and designated at the time of their appointment that the term of one member shall expire in three years, one in two years, and one in one year. The full term of office thereafter shall be for three years, and all vacancies occurring shall be filled by the governor, with the advice and consent of the council. The members of said board may be removed by the governor, with the advice and consent of the council, for such cause as he shall deem sufficient and shall express in the order of removal. They shall each receive in full compensation for their services an annual salary of two thousand dollars, payable in equal monthly instalments, and also their travelling expenses. They may expend annually for clerk hire, engineers, and for defraying expenses incidental to and necessary for the performance of their duties, exclusive of office rent, the sum of two thousand dollars. They shall be provided with an office in the State-house or some other suitable place in the city of Boston, in which the records of their office shall be kept. They may establish rules and regulations for the conduct of business and for carrying out the provisions of this act.

SEC. 2. They shall from time to time compile statistics relating to the public roads of cities, towns, and counties, and make such investigations relating thereto as they shall deem expedient. They may be consulted at all reasonable times, without charge, by officers of counties, cities, or towns, having the care of and authority over public roads, and shall without charge advise them relative to the construction, repair, alteration, or maintenance of the same; but advice given by them to any such officers shall not impair the legal duties and obligations of any county, city, or town. They shall prepare a map or maps of the Commonwealth, on which shall be shown county, city, and town boundaries and also the public roads, particularly the State highways, giving, when practicable, the names of the same. They shall collect and collate information concerning the geological formation of this Commonwealth, so far as it relates to the material suitable and proper for road-building, and shall, so far as practicable, designate on said map or maps the location of such material. Such map or maps shall at all reasonable times be open for the inspection of officers of counties, cities, and towns having the care of and authority over public roads. They shall each year hold at least one public meeting in each county for the open discussion of questions

Statistics.

Map.

relating to the public roads, due notice of which shall be given in the press or otherwise.

Annual report. SEC. 3. They shall make an annual report to the legislature of their doings and the expenditures of their office, together with such statements, facts, and explanations bearing upon the construction and maintenance of public roads, and such suggestions and recommendations as to the general policy of the Commonwealth in respect to the same, as may seem to them appropriate. Their report shall be transmitted to the secretary of the Commonwealth on or before the first Wednesday in January of each year, to be laid before the legislature. All maps, plans, and statistics collected and compiled under their direction shall be preserved in their office.

Information. SEC. 4. County commissioners and city and town officers having the care and authority over public roads and bridges throughout the Commonwealth shall, on request, furnish the commissioners any information required by them concerning the roads and bridges within their jurisdiction.

Expenses. SEC. 5. For the purpose of carrying out the provisions of this act said commission may expend such sums for necessary assistants, the procuring of necessary supplies, instruments, material, machinery, and other property, and for the construction and maintenance of State highways, as shall from time to time be appropriated by the legislature; and they shall in their annual report state what sums they deem necessary for the year commencing with the first day of March following.

Acquisition of new State highways. SEC. 6. Whenever the county commissioners of a county adjudge that the common necessity and convenience require that the Commonwealth acquire as a State highway a new or an existing road in that county, they may apply by petition in writing to the Massachusetts Highway Commission, stating the road they recommend, and setting forth a detailed description of said road by metes and bounds, together with a plan and profile of the same. Said commission shall consider such petition, and if they adjudge that it ought to be allowed, they shall in writing so notify said county commissioners. It shall then become the duty of said county commissioners to cause said road to be surveyed and laid out in the manner provided for the laying out and alteration of highways, the entire expense thereof to be borne and paid by said county. Said county commissioners shall preserve a copy of such petition, plans, and profiles with their record for public inspection. When said commission shall be satisfied that said county commissioners have properly surveyed and laid out said road, and set in place suitable monuments, and have furnished said commission with plans and profiles, on which shall be shown such monuments and established grades, in accordance with the rules and regulations of said commission, said commission may approve the same, and so notify in writing said county commissioners. Said commission shall then present a certified copy of said petition, on which their approval shall be indicated, together with their estimates for constructing said road and the estimated annual cost for maintaining the same, to the secretary of the Commonwealth, who shall at once lay the same before the legislature, if it is in session, otherwise on the second Wednesday of January following. If the legislature makes appropriation for constructing said road, said commission shall cause said road to be constructed in accordance with this act, and when completed and approved by them said road shall become a State highway, and thereafter be maintained by the Commonwealth under the supervision of said commission.

SEC. 7. Two or more cities or towns may petition the said commission representing that, in their opinion, the common necessity and convenience require that the Commonwealth should acquire as a State highway a new or an existing road leading from one city or town to another, which petition shall be accom-

Proceedings in acquiring new State highway.

panied by a detailed description of such road by metes and bounds, and also a plan and profile of the same. If said commission adjudge that the common necessity and convenience require such road to be laid out and acquired as a State highway, they shall cause a copy of said petition, on which shall be their finding, to be given to the county commissioners of the county in which said road or any portion of it lies. It shall then become the duty of the county commissioners, at the expense of the county, to cause said road to be surveyed and laid out, and to set in place suitable monuments, and to cause a detailed description by metes and bounds, plans and profiles, to be made, on which shall be shown said monuments and established grades, and to give the same to said commission; but said county commissioners shall have the right to change the line of said road, provided the termini are substantially the same. Said county commissioners shall preserve said petition and a copy of the plans and profiles, with their records, for public inspection. When said commission shall be satisfied that the county commissioners have properly surveyed and laid out said road and set in place suitable monuments, and have furnished them with plans and profiles on which shall be shown said monuments and established grades, in accordance with the rules and regulations of said commission, they shall then proceed in the same manner as provided in section six of this act; and when said road is completed and approved by said commission it shall become a State highway, and thereafter be maintained by the Commonwealth under the supervision of said commission.

Cost of construction, how paid.

Sec. 8. In all cases where a highway is to be constructed at the expense of the Commonwealth as a State highway, all the grading necessary to make said highway of the established grade, and the construction of culverts and bridges, shall be paid for by the county or counties, respectively, in which said highway or any portion of it lies, and the work must be done to the satisfaction of said commission. No action by a person claiming damage for the taking of land or change of grade, under the provisions of this act, shall be commenced against a county until said commission has taken possession for the purpose of constructing such State highway.

SEC. 9. When appropriation has been made by the legislature for the construction of a State highway, said commission shall at once cause plans and specifications to be made, and estimate the cost of the construction of such State highway, and give to each city and town in which said road lies, a certified copy of said plans and specifications, with a notice that said commission is ready for the construction of said road. Such city or town shall have the right, without advertisement, to contract with said commission for the construction of so much of such highway as lies within its limits, in accordance with the plans and specifications of the commission and under its supervision and subject to its approval, at a price agreed upon between said commission and said city or town; but such price agreed upon shall not exceed eighty-five per cent of the original estimate of said commission. If such city or town shall within thirty days not elect to so contract, said commission may advertise in one or more papers published in the county where the road or a portion of it is situated, and in one or more papers published in Boston, for bids for the construction of said highway in accordance with the plans and specifications furnished by said commission, and under their supervision and subject to their approval. Said commission shall have the right to reject any and all bids, and they shall require of the contractor a bond for at least ten thousand dollars for each mile of road, to indemnify such city or town in which such highway lies against damage while such road is being constructed, and the Commonwealth shall not be liable for any damage occasioned thereby. Said commission shall make and sign all contracts in the name of the Massachusetts Highway Commission.

Commission may advertise for bids.

Repairs.

SEC. 10. For the maintenance of State highways, said commission shall contract with the city or town in which such State highway lies, or a person, firm, or corporation, for the keeping in repair and maintaining of such highway, in accordance with the rules and regulations of said commission and subject to their supervision and approval, and such contracts may be made without previous advertisement.

Approved.

SEC. 11. All contracts made by or with the Massachusetts Highway Commission under the provisions of this act shall be subject to the approval of the governor and council.

Removal of buildings.

SEC. 12. No length of possession or occupancy of land within the limit of any State highway, by an owner or occupier of adjoining land, shall create a right to such land in any adjoining owner or occupant or a person claiming under him, and any fences, buildings, sheds, or other obstructions encroaching upon such State highway shall, upon written notice by said commission, at once be removed by the owner or occupier of adjoining land, and if not so removed said commission may cause the same to be done and may remove the same upon the adjoining land of such owner or occupier.

Injuries.

SEC. 13. The Commonwealth shall be liable for injuries to persons or property occurring through a defect or want of repair or of sufficient railing in or upon a State highway.

Jurisdiction.

SEC. 14. Cities and towns shall have police jurisdiction over all State highways, and they shall at once notify in writing the State commission or its employés of any defect or want of repair in such highways. No State highway shall be dug up for laying or placing pipes, sewers, posts, wires, railways, or other purposes, and no tree shall be planted or removed or obstruction placed thereon, except by the written consent of the superintendent of streets or road commissioners of a city or town, approved by the highway commission, and then only in accordance with the rules and regulations of said commission; and in all cases the work shall be executed under the supervision and to the satisfaction of said commission, and the entire expense of replacing the highway in as good condition as before shall be paid by the parties to whom the consent was given or by whom the work was done; but a city or town shall have the right to dig up such State highway without such approval of the highway commission where immediate necessity demands it, but in all such cases such highway shall be at once replaced in as good condition as before, and at the expense of the city or town. Said commission shall give suitable names to the State highways, and they shall have the right to change the name of any road that shall have become a part of a State highway. They shall cause to be erected, at convenient points along State highways, suitable guide posts.

SEC. 15. The word "road," as used in this act, includes every thoroughfare which the public has a right to use. *Road defined.*

SEC. 16. This act shall take effect upon its passage. *In effect.*
Approved June 10, 1893.

STATE ENGINEER DEPARTMENT.

LAW PROPOSED BY THE MARYLAND ROAD LEAGUE.

SECTION 1. There shall be appointed by the governor of this State, with the consent and approval of the senate, on March 1, 1894, and every fourth year thereafter, an expert engineer, to be the State road and highway engineer, who shall hold his office for the term of four years or until his successor is appointed.

SEC. 2. He shall receive a salary of $5000 per annum, shall give bond for the faithful discharge of his duties in the amount of $5000, and shall pay over all moneys, papers, etc., at the expiration of his term or when ordered by the governor.

SEC. 3. It shall be the duty of the attorney-general, at the request of the governor, to give his counsel and opinion to such officer.

Sec. 4. He shall be provided with suitable offices and working equipment, and is hereby empowered to employ such engineers, clerks, and other assistants, at such salaries as the board of public works may, upon his application, approve.

Sec. 5. He shall submit to the governor on or before January 1, 1896, and every two years thereafter, a report upon the state of the roads and bridges in the State and the best methods of constructing and maintaining the same, with estimates of cost, expenses, etc., and shall suggest some general plan of administration thereof, either by the State or counties, or jointly, or such changes in the present methods as may recommend themselves to him.

Sec. 6. He shall further, upon the application of any of the county boards of highways and bridges herein provided for, give them the benefit of his advice, counsel, and assistance, either in person or by deputy.

Sec. 7. He shall further, upon the application of any such board, detail an assistant engineer to assist it in its work for such time as may be proper, provided all the expenses incurred by such assistant in such work over and above his personal expenses and salary shall be paid for by such board.

Sec. 8. He is further empowered, with the approval of the board of public works, to purchase stone-breaking machines, to set them up at convenient points, and to supply stone to the county boards at cost price.

Sec. 9. He shall render to the governor, legislature, and board of public works such other services as they may require.

Sec. 10. He shall keep a record of all his proceedings and an account of all money received and spent and for what purpose, which record and account he shall furnish to the governor on the 1st day of July each and every year; such records and accounts, however, to be always open to the inspection of the governor or any committee of the legislature.

Sec. 11. All moneys paid out on account of this department shall be paid out by the State treasurer upon the order of the State engineer, indorsed by the comptroller.

Sec. 12. The sum of $25,000 per annum, or so much thereof as may be needed, is hereby appropriated out of any funds in the treasury for the use of this department.

APPENDIX. 163

FREE ROAD MATERIALS BY CONVICT LABOR.

(1) LAWS OF DELAWARE, CHAPTER 670, 1893.

Within two years from and after the passage of this act the Levy Court of New Castle county are authorized and directed to secure, by purchase or condemnation, as hereinafter provided, a stone quarry along the route or within convenient reach of a railroad in New Castle county, the stone in said quarry to be of a character suitable for being broken into macadam. That the said Levy Court, within the time specified, shall advertise for bids and proposals and grant to the lowest and best bidder the contract for the building of a suitable structure for confining prisoners, the same not to exceed in cost the sum of twenty thousand dollars. *[Levy Court of New Castle county authorized to secure a stone quarry. Location of. Shall contract for a building to confine prisoners. Cost of.]*

SECTION 2. It shall be and may be lawful for any court in New Castle county, having competent jurisdiction in the matters of obtaining money under false pretences, pointing a deadly weapon, carrying concealed a deadly weapon, gambling, lottery, policy writing, assault and battery, assaults, drunkenness, disorderly conduct, and vagrancy, and of such other crimes the punishment for which, in the discretion of the court passing sentence, should be hard labor, to sentence any male person or persons convicted as aforesaid to imprisonment in the workhouse of New Castle county at hard labor in the quarry aforesaid, in addition to the penalties prescribed by law; *provided nevertheless* that such imprisonment at hard labor, for drunkenness, disorderly conduct, and vagrancy shall not exceed sixty days. *[Courts in New Castle county may commit certain offenders to workhouse at hard labor in stone quarry. Imprisonment for drunkenness, etc., not to exceed sixty days.]*

SECTION 3. It shall be the duty of the superintendent of the workhouse hereinafter provided for to receive all persons who may be sentenced under the *[Duty of superintendent of workhouse.]*

provisions of Section 2 of this act and keep them at hard labor as herein provided.

Who to be deemed vagrants under this act.

SECTION 4. That all beggars and vagabonds who roam about from place to place, without any lawful business or occupation, sleeping in outhouses, barns, market places, sheds, and in the open air, and not giving a good account of themselves, shall be deemed vagrants and liable to the penalties of this act.

Eight hours a day's work.

Working hours.

No exemption from labor except for physical inability.

Management of refractory prisoners.

Action of superintendent to be reported to jail commissioners.

SECTION 5. Eight hours shall constitute a day's work at hard labor, and such hard labor shall be performed between the hours of eight o'clock in the morning and five o'clock in the evening. No person sentenced under this act shall be exempt from said labor except through physical inability properly certified to the superintendent of the workhouse by the jail physician. Should any prisoners prove refractory and stubborn, and refuse to work or perform his or their work in a proper manner, the superintendent of the workhouse shall have power to place such prisoner or prisoners in solitary confinement, there to be kept on bread and water until he or they shall submit to perform his or their tasks and to obey his orders. Every action of the superintendent under this section shall be reported immediately to the jail commissioners, who shall have power to revise the same.

Duty of jail commissioners respecting government of workhouse.

SECTION 12. The commissioners of the jail and workhouse shall have power to make rules for the government of the workhouse and all persons connected therewith, for the cleanliness and health of the prisoners, and for the employment of convicts; they shall have power to order fuel and bedding, to furnish working tools, materials, and fixtures for the workhouse, and, when directed by the levy court, they may purchase such stone-breaking machinery as the said levy court may deem proper and expedient, and to erect such buildings and walls as may be ordered by the levy court.

Condemnation of quarry;

SECTION 13. Should the levy court fail to secure the quarry aforesaid by purchase, then they shall proceed to secure some suitable quarry by applying to the Court of General Sessions of the Peace and Jail Delivery of the State of Delaware in and for New Castle county for the appointment of five suitable persons, who shall go upon and view the premises selected by the levy court aforesaid and proceed to condemn the same under the law and in the manner provided for the condemnation of land for road or county purposes in Chapter 60, Revised Code of the State of Delaware. *[how to be effected.]*

SECTION 14. The stone shall be broken so that it can be used for road macadam. The stone so broken shall be divided among the several hundreds of New Castle county making demand therefor and upon payment by such hundreds of the costs of transportation. *[Stone, how broken.]*

The division shall be made in the following manner, that is to say: should the supply exceed the demands of the several hundreds, the said hundreds shall be entitled to receive any quantity that may be ordered by the road commissioners thereof, or the street and sewer department of the City of Wilmington, and the transportation paid therefor, and if in the judgment of the commissioners of the jail and workhouse the supply of stone is much in excess of the demand, they may, after sufficient advertisement, sell the same or a part thereof at public sale, and turn over the proceeds therefrom to the receiver of taxes and county treasurer of New Castle county. Should the demand for stone from the several hundreds be greater than the supply, the stone shall then be equally divided between the several hundreds, car load at a time, until the orders of the several hundreds are filled and the [supply] of stone exhausted. The superintendent of the workhouse shall superintend and manage the breaking of stone, the loading of cars, and the filling of orders of the several hundreds, or purchasers at public sale; and he shall receive all payment therefor, and settle with the county treasurer on the first Monday of every month; such settlements shall be audited by the comptroller of accounts of New Castle county. *[How divided among the hundreds. General provisions in relation to distribution of broken stone.]*

How stone shall be applied to streets and roads by City of Wilmington and the commissioners of the several hundreds.

SECTION 15. The road commissioners of any hundred in New Castle county, or street and sewer department of the City of Wilmington, making demands for stone and receiving the same, shall select one certain road in their hundred to improve, and they shall complete the improvements thereon before stone is put upon any other road. The road shall be graded, macadamized, piked, or otherwise improved by means of stone, for a width of at least twelve feet, whenever such improvement may be required to keep the same constantly in good condition. The improvement of the roads by means of stone, as aforesaid, shall be, as far as practicable, continuous along the entire length of the road.

(2) PROPOSED LAW IN IOWA.

(From *The Clinton Age.*)

Senator Green has a new plan for bettering the roads of the State which is proposed in a bill introduced by him. He proposes that rock for macadamizing the roads and streets of the State shall be furnished from the State quarry at Anamosa. The stone is to be quarried by the convicts, broken into proper size and loaded on cars by them and furnished free of charge to cities and townships whose council or trustees will pay the freight. This, according to the senator's idea, will not only furnish material for the construction of magnificent roads, but will also give ample employment for the State's convict labor.

Not the least important feature of the senator's bill is the taking of convict labor out of competition with paid labor. The *Age* has often declared it were better that prisoners should be employed to do a kind of work one day and undo it the next, rather than to engage in any business which came in competition with paid labor. We believe that Senator Green's plan would work admirably, and that the railroads would haul the material at or below cost. The railroads of Iowa have already shown a disposition to co-operate with the people in carrying out any practical plan of permanent road-building. We hope the Green bill will become a law. We do not know how the prisoners are employed, but we do know that every labor organization in the State ought to immediately pass resolutions favoring the Green bill.

www.ingramcontent.com/pod-product-compliance
Lightning Source LLC
Chambersburg PA
CBHW020925230426
43666CB00008B/1577